Other books by Dan Stark:
Silence of the Bunnies

Tewksbury Tales Press, LLC.
9 Patriot Hill Drive
Basking Ridge, NJ 07920

First Tewksbury edition 2012
Original published in the United States by arrangement with the author.

Book and cover designed by David Stark
Set in Adobe Garamond Pro
Cover illustration by Michael Morgenstern
Manufactured in the United States of America

Library of Congress Control Number: 2012947787
ISBN-13: 978-1-934160-02-2

Tewksbury Tales Press

GELDING GOLIATH

An
Insider's
Account
of the
Destruction
of
AT&T

*This book is dedicated to the
memory of my father, Sid Stark,
who demonstrated that modesty
and brilliance can co-exist in the
corporate world.*

DAN STARK

Table of Contents

(Continued)

Introduction

The former American Telephone and Telegraph Company, for which I worked for twenty-one years, died in 2005. It was bought for chump change by one of the companies it had spawned in 1984 at the time the government broke up the Bell System. Included in the assets purchased was the right to use the AT&T name, and the new company calls itself AT&T. But it is not the same company. This book is about the former AT&T, the company I started out hating and came to love. This is a book that tells the truth about AT&T's destruction, as it only could be told by someone who lived through it.

The word "gelding" refers both to the figurative fate of the company, and the literal fate of the statue that came to represent it. Cast in bronze in 1914, the giant twenty-eight foot statue was covered with more than forty thousand pieces of gold leaf. Originally called "The Genius of Electricity," it was renamed by AT&T in the mid-1930s "The Spirit of Communications," and came to symbolize the company. It was known to employees simply as "Golden Boy."

Golden Boy began its life perched 29 stories high on the roof of AT&T headquarters at 195 Broadway in New York City. In 1984, it moved to the foyer of AT&T's new headquarters building at 550 Madison Ave. Concerned that the giant statue's anatomical accuracy would offend passers-by who would now be "up close and personal" with it, then Chairman John de Butts ordered the statue gelded. It was in this reduced state that the statue moved first to Basking Ridge, New Jersey in 1992 (when the building at 550 Madison Avenue was sold to Sony), then to Bedminister, New Jersey in 2002 (when the Basking Ridge complex was sold), and finally to Dallas, Texas in 2009, to the new AT&T corporate headquarters.

There is nothing remarkable about companies failing – it happens all the time. But there was something shocking about AT&T's demise, because it had been the most powerful company in the world, and one whose technological leadership, market position, and cash generation put it so far ahead of its rivals that it seemingly was invulnerable to the slings and arrows of normal corporate combat.

In its prime, AT&T was a company beyond compare, a corporation with a government-sanctioned monopoly over phone service so profitable that its income in 1970, for instance, exceeded the incomes for the same period of General Motors, Ford, General Electric, and IBM combined. Its revenues, compared to the entire economies of the world's largest countries, would have put it in eighth place. AT&T was viewed as the perfect can't-fail investment for widows and orphans, paying dividends without fail for over one hundred years. You want a safe investment? Put your money in "T."

Joseph Nacchio, at the time an AT&T executive, liked to say that there was only one other business that came close to AT&T's core long distance business in profitability (i.e., narcotics), but the other business was illegal. AT&T offered local service through twenty-two local telephone companies, serving virtually every desirable market in the country. Long distance service was offered through a centralized entity called "AT&T Long Lines." All of these operations were monopolies, and fantastically, consistently profitable.

In addition to the services business, the Bell System, as AT&T was known, had two other key units. The first was Western Electric, the largest manufacturer of telecom equipment in the world. Western

Electric made every piece of telecom equipment necessary to construct a telephone network, from those ubiquitous black telephones that sat on customer desks and seemed to last forever to the most sophisticated voice networking products in the world. Western made in U.S. factories the big network switches that routed calls from place to place, and the medium—be it trans-oceanic cables, satellites, fiber, copper, or digital radio—to get it there.

The third critical part of AT&T was Bell Laboratories (or "Bell Labs" or simply "the labs"). Many other companies concentrate their personnel whose function it is to come up with new products into research and development entities. But Bell Labs was much more. Of its more than twenty-thousand employees, the Labs had more than eleven hundred employees dedicated to basic research, that is, research aimed at improving our general understanding of the world around us, without an immediate profit motivation. Even after the advent of competition made it much more cost conscious, AT&T still spent more than three hundred million dollars a year on basic research.

There is no other corporation in the world that has ever come close to this commitment to research, nor is there any institution that has changed life on our planet as significantly as Bell Labs did with its dizzying array of inventions. Had it invented nothing other than the transistor, which it did in 1947, AT&T would have been entitled to make that claim, for the transistor has moved mankind into the "Information Age," and is widely regarded as the most significant invention of the twentieth century. But Bell Labs did so much more, inventing the laser; designing, building and launching the first communications satellite (Telstar); inventing the computer language that underlies the internet (Unix); inventing virtually every communications technology used today (including fiber optics, cellular telephony, digital switching and digital radio); inventing digital signal processors; solar cells; and discovering the wave theory of matter and the Big Bang theory of the creation of the universe. In all, AT&T won eight Nobel prizes for work done at Bell Labs.

In short, AT&T was a company that couldn't be described without using superlatives. It was at one point or another the largest corporation, with the most revenues, profits, and assets of any company in the world, employing over a million people, and producing the most incredible litany of inventions and innovations of any entity in the world!

Yet the company's fortunes fell so far so fast that by the time of its demise in 2005, its purchase for scrap value by a competitor was barely considered newsworthy, and in fact is overlooked by many who are unaware it even happened.

I joined AT&T in July 1983 as an attorney, after working six years in private practice in Washington D.C. Over the course of the next twenty-one years, I worked my way up to become an officer and one of AT&T's top lawyers. As the Chief Counsel for AT&T's Business Services Group (about $28 billion in annual revenues), AT&T's Network Operations Group, and the International Operations Group, there was little that happened of which I was unaware. I was deeply involved in the long and painful fight, which we lost, to save the company from itself and its external enemies.

Some of the people I met during my time with AT&T were truly exceptional. I worked with, and have great respect for, John Zeglis, Dave Dorman, Chuck Noski, Gail McGovern, Bill Marx, Hossein Eslambolchi, Jim Cicconi, Frank Ianna, Hal Burlingame, Dan Schulman, Michael Keith, Betsy Bernard, Jeff Weitzen, Ken Sichau, Dick Martin, Bill Hannigan, Reed Harrison, Dan Sheinbein, Bob

Aqualina, MJ McKeever, Cliff Holtz, Barb Peda, Tim Murray, John Haigh, and Gerry Salemme.[1]

This is not their book. Rather, this book focuses on those who made the catastrophic decisions that *helped* bring down the greatest company in the world. These were not small errors; these were colossal blunders, at times aggravated by the extreme arrogance of those making them.

I say "helped" because no matter how foolish the acts of management it would have been impossible to bring down AT&T unless it first had been weakened by the one "person" who could have made the company vulnerable: Uncle Sam. Prior to Uncle Sam's actions, no amount of company mismanagement could have hurt AT&T seriously. Lose a billion dollars? No problem! Increase prices for long distance service by a fraction of a cent and you've got it back and more! The fact that AT&T had so outdistanced its rivals meant it had a license to print money. Before the acts of management could affect the company, its ability to immunize itself from the consequences of even colossal blunders had to be destroyed. This was no small matter, even for Uncle Sam. It took five decades of government malfeasance to render AT&T mortal.

Why did I write this book? There's already a plethora of other accounts about various aspects of the rise and fall of the Bell System. None, however, capture what I call the "Colossal Failures" that broke AT&T's back, nor the role of government in taking advantage of a weakened company to put it in a fatal predicament. There are only a small group of people who were close enough to what was going

---

1. The list is not meant to be exhaustive. There are a number of other fine individuals not mentioned either because our paths didn't cross much, or because their names would only be meaningful to their mothers. I also didn't include my fellow lawyers. We had so many good ones that their inclusion would have overwhelmed the rest of the list.

on inside the company, and understood what they were witnessing both from legal and business perspectives to have written an accurate account. I am the only one of that small group to try to do so. Were I a modest man, I would not claim my book to be more accurate than the other accounts I have seen. But I'm not, and it is. So sit back and enjoy your fly-on-the-wall status while I try to recreate what happened to the greatest company in the world.

It is said that the victors write the history books. Not this one! I write with a profound sense of loss for what might have been, and ask forgiveness in advance if a little emotion creeps into the narrative. I spent twenty-one years working for AT&T, representing the better part of my professional career. It was an incredible journey. "Ma Bell" was quite a lady: cantankerous, brilliant and at times, idiotic. God bless her, I'm going to miss the old bitch. And all of us, whether we know it or not, are going to miss Bell Labs.

Chapter 1

The Beginnings of My AT&T Career

I was an unlikely candidate to become an AT&T loyalist and insider. I had started my legal career in 1977 (following my graduation from Boston University School of Law) at a small firm in Washington D.C., called at the time Cole, Zylstra and Raywid. It primarily represented cable television companies before the Federal Communications Commission (or "FCC"). Alan Raywid was a romantic who loved tilting at windmills. His passion was to represent "underdogs" in their fights against the establishment. He ran a small litigation group at the firm, and I was hired to work for him.

When I joined, Raywid was preparing for an antitrust trial *against* AT&T on behalf of Hiram King, a litigious small businessman who had tried to build a cable television system in Aberdeen, South Dakota. AT&T had turned down King's request to lash his cables to the telephone poles there, so King tried to build an underground system in the middle of the South Dakota winter. In the battle of backhoes versus the frozen ground, the ground most frequently prevailed. King's business failed, in part because of the higher than expected construction costs, and in part due to his own business ineptitude. He had previously sued the power company for "sight pollution," and I suspect he would have gone happily away at the beginning of the case for a few thousand dollars.

That changed when AT&T as part of the discovery process turned over documents prepared by a mid-level competitive analyst named Norm Pullen. Pullen had prepared the documents as a vu-graph presentation, meaning the words were few and one had to get right to the point, without the usual equivocation found in many corporate records. Pullen seemed to be trying to rouse the company from complacency to what he saw as the threat to AT&T from cable systems. Describing the coaxial cables being deployed to homes by cable systems as "noses under the tent," he warned prophetically that there were already millions of such noses. Pullen wrote, "We must own the pipes. Not just own them, but control them." This document, more than any other, revealed that AT&T viewed cable systems as a competitive threat, making it reasonable to test the company's behavior under antitrust standards.

AT&T tried to do something about cable systems in the late 1970's, implementing "safety" practices which limited non-AT&T cable attachments to one per pole (the policy pursuant to which King's request was denied). For those who couldn't get attachments or didn't want to build their own system, AT&T offered its own "channel service" whereby someone wanting to get into the business would lease AT&T-owned facilities to offer service to its customers. That way, AT&T would own the pipes and cable companies would merely provide the content. The cable industry, however, frustrated the AT&T initiative, getting a court to agree with it that Section 214 of the Communications Act required Federal Communication Commission ("FCC") approval before AT&T could offer such service. Then, each time AT&T would try to offer the service, the cable industry would intervene in the FCC proceeding, challenging the offering as contrary to the public interest, tying AT&T up in regulatory proceedings until the potential customer for the service abandoned it for some other solution.

I joined the trial team my first week as a lawyer, not because Raywid thought I was a genius, but because I was the only litigation associate willing to go to Rapid City, South Dakota, for the three months necessary to try the case. I had neither children nor pets at the time that might miss me. I drove Raywid's beaten-up BMW cross-country to Rapid City, pulling a U-Haul filled with our documents. Our team consisted of Raywid and myself, our local counsel (a delightful man named Joe Butler who made us laugh almost constantly), and Fran Chetwynd, a New Zealand-born attorney who stayed in D.C. but helped with the brief writing.

AT&T had two large law firms (Sidley & Austin and Faegre & Benson) working on the case, in addition to local counsel and a substantial contingent of in-house AT&T attorneys. One of the corporate jets would fly important people in and out on a daily basis.[2] I remember Bill Ellinghaus, the AT&T President, being one of those to fly in the day he was to testify. AT&T routinely had about eight to ten lawyers in court, and my estimate is they had twice that number working on the case.

Fortuitous for my career, John Zeglis, the future General Counsel at AT&T was one of the Sidley & Austin attorneys who helped at trial. He was the protégé of Howard Trienens, then AT&T's General Counsel and still a partner at the same law firm. When Trienens wanted to retire from AT&T, he brought Zeglis in at an "entry level" job as a Vice President. Zeglis was then elevated to General Counsel when Trienens left, the latter returning to Sidley & Austin.[3]

---

2 Concerned about the impact the arrival of the corporate jet would have on the judge, AT&T sent teams to re-open an old Air Force strip about thirty miles away from Rapid City. The move backfired as the question of what AT&T was doing opening up the old Air Force base became the talk of the town.

3 Zeglis' path to be the General Counsel may have been eased by Trienens, but none who knew Zeglis ever doubted his credentials for the job. In addition to being the smartest attorney I encountered during my career, he also had an intense competitive spirit that permeated his every action. Even his Christmas parties became competitive events, with table pitted against table in various games.

Concerned that a jury trial would take too long and that we would run out of funds,[4] Raywid had agreed to waive our client's right to a jury trial. We therefore tried the case to the judge. Judge Andrew Bogue was not a romantic, nor frankly was he interested in rocking the boat. His main job in Rapid City seemed to be sentencing native-Americans who would get drunk, steal a car, and then abandon it when they concluded that they had too much to drink, and really ought to stop driving. (Because criminal sentencing took precedence over civil litigation, our trial would be interrupted almost every day to enable Judge Bogue to deal with these petty offenses.) He would lecture them about private property, they would hang their heads and apologize with great sincerity, and then the whole thing would be repeated a few days later. Perhaps the entire community was hard drinking, but these were American Indians and unlike their non-Indian compatriots, their transgressions fell within the jurisdiction of the federal courts. Thus, each morning before our case would proceed, the assembled lawyers would sit and watch the sentencing of American Indians on alcohol-related charges.[5]

Our case was fairly simple. We sought to prove that AT&T had denied our client access to an "essential facility" – i.e., utility poles - as part of an anticompetitive plan to limit competition from cable television entities, and that this had directly injured our client by raising his costs. AT&T's defense was equally simple – cable television utilized a primitive one-way network, incapable of supporting the delivery of

---

4 The law firm had taken the case on a contingent fee basis, meaning we would only be paid if we won. Additionally, even the out of pocket costs of running the litigation were being absorbed by Raywid's firm, since the plaintiff lacked the funds to cover them.

5 State courts typically deal with criminal matters. Federal courts are much fewer in number and handle only such matters as Congress, or the Constitution, delegates to them – such as alleged violations of federal laws, or certain matters regarding Indians.

services competitive with those offered by AT&T, and therefore there was no antitrust violation because the two companies, TV Signal of Aberdeen (our client) and the American Telephone and Telegraph Company (the defendant), were not competitors.[6]

Judge Bogue issued a written decision a few months after the trial concluded, in AT&T's favor. The decision tracked the AT&T arguments, and even contained some of the same typographical errors as AT&T's proposed findings of fact and conclusions of law. It was a depressing time, and we nearly didn't pursue an appeal.

It is tough to successfully appeal a decision based on a factual record. Appellate judges are extremely reluctant to overrule such decisions, because they have not had the chance to watch the witnesses, check their demeanor, and tell who has been naughty and who has been nice. Perhaps it was the long-shot nature of the appeal, or perhaps he had been impressed by my performance in trial court, but Raywid supported my request to argue the appeal, even though I was less than a year out of law school and this was the single biggest case the law firm had.

The appeal was held in St. Paul, Minnesota before three federal appellate judges. As the petitioner, we went first. I was nervous until the first question hit, which happened about ten seconds into my argument. I could tell from the judges' questions that they wanted concessions from me that certain things would limit our damages. I viewed this

---

6 In addition to AT&T officials such as William Ellinghaus, AT&T used a variety of "expert" witnesses with impeccable credentials to make its case. Because of cost concerns, we had no such experts. Raywid tried to pooh-pooh the AT&T experts in his arguments, and largely ignored them while they were testifying on direct, raising few objections during their testimony. To further demonstrate their lack of importance, he had me, a few months out of law school, handle their cross examinations. The first witness I ever cross-examined was Eugene Rostow, an economist and former Secretary of State. He took me to school.

as a positive, since we had lost on liability without reaching damages, and the only reason they might be interested on damage issues was because they were thinking of reversing Judge Bogue on liability. I therefore readily made the concessions, and they appeared satisfied. John French, a seasoned appellate lawyer, argued the case for AT&T. To my mind, he didn't read the judges well at all. He didn't get the significance of the judge's questions of me, which should have been a red flag for him to go back and underscore his arguments on liability. Instead, he spent the bulk of his time telling the court about the appropriate standard of review, a waste of his time. (Judges may cite to a limited standard of review to buttress their decision, but rarely rely on it in deciding cases.) I thought we had done well, and was pleased – a feeling that lasted until I spoke to Raywid. He didn't like the fact that I had made concessions on damages, and didn't seem able to see why I felt good about the day.

Waiting for the decision was torture, but worth it. I don't think I've ever equaled the feeling of professional elation I had reading the appellate court's decision, which reversed Judge Bogue three votes to nothing, and made it clear upon remand that the only question the court was leaving open was the amount of damages AT&T owed. With respect to damages, the decision noted the concessions I had made, but it didn't really matter. I had read the court correctly, and we had lived to fight another day! Moreover, under the antitrust laws, AT&T now would have to compensate us for every one of the thousands of hours of attorney time we had spent on the case. For a small firm, that alone was huge!

The case ultimately settled. I moved on before it did, however, leaving Cole, Zylstra & Raywid over a salary dispute. The firm did not pay its associates well, which I understood. It wasn't a wealthy firm. But I nonetheless thought a one thousand dollar raise in annual salary from $17,500 to $18,500, after I had played a significant role in winning the case and the firm stood to collect about three quarters of a million dollars in legal fees, was a bit tight-fisted. My dissatisfaction became more pronounced when I learned that the son of one of the senior partners, a lazy undergraduate who spent his time trying to hit on his father's very pretty secretary, had been hired as a summer clerk and made more per hour than I did. The firm's partners said some things I didn't like; I said some things they didn't like, and I left in 1980 to become an associate at a larger D.C. firm, Dickstein, Shapiro and Morin.[7] This firm had started out as a plaintiff's firm, winning a huge victory over a number of pharmaceutical companies for price-fixing of tetracycline, but had made the transition to representing mostly defendants. There was something to be said for working for clients who had the funds to pay high hourly rates, win, lose or draw.

I worked in the firm's litigation group, under the tutelage of David Shapiro, an outrageous and uncouth man, but one hell of a trial lawyer. Shapiro was on his third marriage, and complained that my colleague and friend Peter Morgan loved his wife too much because Peter had insisted on taking a night off, I think for his anniversary. But what a trial lawyer Shapiro was! I remember his advice that in a trial to a jury you at least once should turn your back to the jury and scratch your butt, so that the jurors know you are just like them. It worked for him. He was not a blue-blooded, refined litigator. He ate those types for lunch.

---

7 Notwithstanding the money, I was lucky to begin my career at Cole, Zylstra & Raywid. The experience I got at a small firm was so much better than I would have gotten at a large one. In addition to the case against AT&T, I also worked on a case involving a boat sinking in the Bermuda triangle, and the defense of Senator Proxmire in the U.S. Supreme Court for giving his "golden fleece" award to a researcher who gave electric shocks to animals and then measured how much they clenched their jaws in response. (The researcher sold the same study to a number of different agencies.) The firm also had an awesome softball team that won the Communications Law title two years in a row, thanks in large part to a great friend, Izzie Rodriquez, our office manager and shortstop.

I was more or less happily learning my trade working round the clock, seven days a week. That's the way it went; we were preparing for an antitrust trial and I was a young associate. I remember one incident that began while I was on the road in Atlanta, Georgia, looking for documents. I was handed a message that Shapiro was trying to reach me. I found a phone and called him. He asked in his gruff voice when I could get to New York City, where he was staying in an apartment the firm maintained there. It was then nearly seven in the evening, and I began to say that I'd take the first flight in the morning, when he interrupted, saying, "I meant tonight, fuck-face." He used his nickname for me without rancor or ill will. But the message was clear. Something was afoot, or so it appeared.

With heroic efforts, I caught a late flight and arrived at the apartment around one in the morning. My knocking must have woken him up, and he answered the door in his boxers, looking a bit bleary-eyed. I waited expectantly for him to reveal what had happened to require my presence that night. He looked at me, rubbed his stomach through his tee shirt, and asked, "You think I'm fat?" He was, but I don't remember saying anything clever in response. I do remember him saying that he was going to bed, offering his sofa as a place for me to sleep. It was late and I had nowhere else to go. I went home the following morning, and then turned around and returned to New York the following day. I had scheduled another document search, this one at the Brooklyn Naval Yard.

I relate that story here because Shapiro, without meaning to (I think), shaped me more than any other mentor or teacher. He exuded power, and knew it. He certainly had power over me, demonstrated by demanding I travel late at night not because it was really necessary but on his caprice. He had power over others because he could cast a spell in courtrooms that tantalized judges and juries alike. He was a force of nature, and presented a tough question to someone who mistakenly had assumed he could enjoy both career and family: did I want to be like him?

Most people find it impossible to comprehend how hard young associates work. I had three days off in six months, and that included weekends and my "honeymoon." I had been in deposition until seven o'clock the night before my wedding. I was young and naïve; I had mistakenly told opposing counsel earlier that afternoon about my upcoming nuptials in the hope that we could expedite what I viewed as a truly unimportant deposition. We might have finished by four o'clock otherwise, but he did his best to drag it out.

My son was born in January 1983, and my wife began raising questions about what kind of father I wanted to be, or could be, in my present job. Holding my son's chubby little body convinced me that there was some other purpose in life than to work. I decided I did not want to be like Shapiro, a workaholic on his third marriage. I answered an advertisement in the Wall Street Journal for a "major NY-based telecom company" looking for attorneys. The company turned out to be AT&T, and the job seemed perfect. I had been working on some AT&T matters at the law firm, and at least those AT&T attorneys I knew didn't work nearly as hard as I did. Better still, they were offering a twenty percent increase in my base pay, great benefits such as free phones and free telephone service, and a superb relocation package that would give me a profit rather than the loss I deserved on the condo I owned in Washington D.C.[8]

When Shapiro learned that I was planning to leave, he tracked me down to the motel where I was staying while doing a final round of interviews. He told me in his gruff voice that I was making the biggest mistake of my life, and that within three years I would be bored out of my mind, and divorced. He was wrong. As AT&T morphed into a competitive company, the work became both intense and interesting. With respect to my personal life, it took *four* years for my wife and me to get divorced. I never did find a satisfactory way to balance career and family, and too often put my job first.

I started working at AT&T on July 1, 1983. The company was in the throes of implementing the settlement of the latest government anti-trust case against the company. This settlement had been signed in January 1982, but was to be implemented on January 1, 1984. It was called the Modification of Final Judgment, or MFJ, and required the company to be split into eight companies: a new AT&T, and seven Regional Bell Operating Companies, or "RBOCs." The world was about to change in ways that no one involved could have guessed.

---

8 My wife and I bought a condo near 22nd and P streets. It was dark on two of four walls because the windows were blocked by other buildings, but was close enough to work so that I could walk the five blocks separating home from office. The asking price had been $92,000. It was my first real estate purchase, and not knowing what I should do, I simply told "my" agent that, "We'll take it." The agent never said a word to the effect that one never offered the asking price. Naturally, our offer was accepted and we bought a two-bedroom apartment in a bad building that would have been difficult to sell at anything close to the price we had paid, but for the AT&T relocation package. Pre-divestiture, that package included buying your existing home at a generous valuation, moving expenses, closing costs of the new residence, and per diems to cover whatever restaurant or other bills one might have during the move. It was good to work for a monopoly!

Chapter 2

There Once Was A Company Called AT&T

Those not familiar with AT&T may be puzzled by the description of it having failed. After all, one can look at the stock page and still find it listed by the simple ticker symbol "T" for telephone. Its advertisements grace the airwaves; AT&T seems to be doing better than ever. It is, except for one thing: the company I am writing about is not the same company referred to in all of those public forums. I am writing about the "real AT&T," the American Telephone and Telegraph Company, founded by Alexander Graham Bell in 1885. Bell invented the telephone and phonograph himself; his company pioneered virtually all of the advances in telecommunications throughout the 20th century. *That* was the real AT&T.

The current "AT&T" is in fact one of the seven companies AT&T spun off in 1984, as required by the Modification of Final Judgment. It originally was called Southwestern Bell Corporation, but changed this to SBC. SBC won the telephone wars and bought Ameritech, Pacific Telesis and Bell South (three other companies divested by AT&T), and AT&T itself. Along with the network and other assets, SBC acquired the rights to the name "AT&T" and sometimes calls itself that or even "at&t." But it is not the same company as the old AT&T. The new company is headquartered in Dallas, Texas; the old company was based for most of its existence in New York City. The company that once shared a hometown culture with Leonard Bernstein, Woody Allen and the Radio City Rockettes now shares one instead with the Dallas Cowboys Cheerleaders. That is neither bad nor good; but it clearly is different.

The new AT&T seems of two minds about whether to embrace the AT&T legacy. For instance, its web pages proudly celebrate the history of Bell Labs as if it were its own history. At the same time, however, the company excludes from its lists of retired officers those who worked at the Labs or other parts of AT&T, listing only those who worked for some period for SBC. The company seemingly is not bothered by the inconsistency of claiming the accomplishments while not acknowledging the people who produced them.

At its core, the old AT&T was a regulated monopoly. It was founded in 1885 on the strength of Alexander Graham Bell's two patents, which were upheld by the Supreme Court by a 5-4 margin, after a race to the patent office with Elijah Grey, the founder of Western Electric. Both men had been working on the telephone, and the challenge to Bell's patents was well financed (backed as it was by the very powerful Western Union). Bell escaped by the narrowest of margins, the court finding that he had made his filing just before that of Elijah Grey.

Bell was an extraordinary and interesting man, who invented both the telephone and the phonograph in connection with his work with the deaf. His father also was a teacher of phonetics and was the role model used by George Bernard Shaw for Professor Higgins in his play Pygmalion (known to most by its popular modern iteration, "My Fair Lady.") Bell originally was from Scotland. He immigrated to Canada in 1870 following the death of his brother from tuberculosis, and moved to Boston, Massachusetts in 1871. In 1876, at the age of 29, he invented the telephone, uttering those famous words over his new invention, "Watson, come here. I want you."

Over time, Bell's company amassed local telephone companies that served most of the desirable markets in the country. This came neither easily or quickly. AT&T didn't have the money necessary to build out the networks necessary to serve the markets open to it, and at one point Bell put his patents up for sale to the dominant telegraph company of the day, Western Union.

It is clear that Western Union turned down his offer. What is less clear is why. Most historians point to a committee report to the Western Union board, which ridiculed the Bell patents, making Western Union appear to have sized things up terribly:

"Mssrs. Hubbard and Bell want to install one of their telephone devices in every city. The idea is idiotic on the face of it. Furthermore, why would any person want to use this ungainly and impractical device when he can send a clear written message to any large city in the United States?"

Western Union may just have been ahead of its time. Most teenagers today would seem to agree with the preference of text over voice, at least if the statement were broadened to refer to "texting" as well as sending a telegraph. At the time it was written, however, the report was supposed to show how badly Western Union had gauged the direction technology would take the market. But, as Dick Martin, AT&T's former head of Public Relations pointed out to me, the report may be a fabrication. The addressee, listed as the Western Union President, didn't hold that position at all. He was instead a member of the Board, something you'd think that the supposed authors of the report would know. In addition, the report is inconsistent with the fact that it was Western Union that had bankrolled the legal challenge to the patents, something it would have been less likely to do if it really had thought the technology to be as silly as the report indicates. Whatever the reason, however, the result was that Western Union stuck with the telegraph, and rode this once-dominant technology into relative obscurity.

Today, one can still send a telegraph, but this mode of communication is almost entirely superseded.[9]

AT&T, on the other hand, took off under the leadership of Theodore Vail, brought in by some of the company's large investors as President in 1907. It was Vail who initiated several national advertising campaigns, introducing in 1908 what was to become the company mantra for the next seventy years: "One System. One Policy. Universal Service." The company began expanding rapidly, utilizing the Bell patents during their seventeen-year lifetimes to prevent others from building telephone networks. After the patents expired, it used the threat of a refusal to interconnect networks with smaller rivals to force the acquisition of systems it wanted.

At the time, the idea of one ubiquitous network where anyone could call anyone else was still a dream. While companies would permit anyone they "wired up" to call any of their other customers, the interconnections stopped there; a customer of one company could not call a customer of any other company. The absence of interconnection between telephone companies meant that an individual wanting to call another individual either had to belong to the same "network," or had to have a phone tied into the network the called customer utilized. A business, for example, would have to have multiple telephones if it wanted the ability to call anyone – and many telephone customers did have two or three or sometimes even more phones sitting on their desks, using whichever phone was necessary to reach the person they desired. This environment lasted until the Communications Act of 1934, which gave the newly created Federal Communications Commission the authority to not only require interconnection of all networks but to specify the terms and conditions governing such interconnections.

---

9 Texting or emailing is so much easier than sending a telegraph that Western Union, in order to survive, has had to focus on certain niche applications, such as wiring funds from one person to another.

In 1913, AT&T signed the Kingsbury Commitment, settling the government's first antitrust suit against it. The agreement sanctioned the company as a regulated monopoly, and allowed it to acquire independent telephone companies so long as it divested the same number. In exchange, the company agreed to divest Western Union's telegraph business (which it had acquired) and to permit interconnection of independent companies to the company's long distance network.

The same year, AT&T purchased Lee de Forest's vacuum tubes patent, and the rights to the first three-element vacuum tube. Vacuum tubes had the capability to greatly amplify telephone signals. The purchase of this technology gave AT&T a position of real dominance in long distance communications. Now legally, the company became the only one that could offer telephone service over long distances with good quality.

Walter Gifford, the next president of AT&T, decided to focus the company almost exclusively on achieving universal service – the notion that everyone who wanted a phone should have one – in this country. The company had begun selling its telephone equipment around the world, which Gifford viewed as a distraction. The market positions that were sold off as a "distraction" would later have been incredibly valuable when AT&T sought to compete globally, and included manufacturing entities in France and Germany (IT&T) and Japan (NEC).

In 1925, AT&T formed a research entity that it called "Bell Laboratories," which won the first of its eight Nobel prizes in 1937 for experimental confirmation of the wave theory of matter.

The Communications Act of 1934 established a regulatory framework that is still used (more or less) today. The Act established the Federal Communications Commission (FCC), and gave it numerous powers over interstate communications. The FCC could order carriers to interconnect their networks, and gave the agency the authority to set the terms, including compensation, governing such interconnections. It also prohibited carriers from discriminating amongst their customers, and required all such rates to be included in tariffs filed with the FCC and to be "just and reasonable."

AT&T flourished, introducing innovation after innovation. In 1919, it introduced dial telephones, which enabled customers to establish the call path without the use of an operator. In 1922, AT&T started the first commercial radio service; and in 1927, it demonstrated the first television service, taking live pictures of then Commerce Secretary Herbert Hoover in Washington, D.C. and showing them to an audience in New York. Also in 1927, AT&T began the first transatlantic telephone service between the U.S. and London, costing $75 for the first three minutes. In 1948, it introduced broadcast services so that television networks could broadcast shows throughout the country. In 1951, it introduced the ability for customers to dial *long distance* calls without the assistance of an operator, and call volumes exploded.

Without regulation, AT&T could have made huge profits. Under the regulatory regime created by Communications Act, however, the FCC established the "rate of return" AT&T was authorized to make on its offerings of interstate services, and AT&T was not permitted to make in excess of that. Similarly, state regulatory commissions set comparable rates of return for intrastate (i.e., calls that did not cross state lines) services, which limited how much the company could make from those services. The rule in both jurisdictions was as follows: the company could recover every dollar of expenses it incurred on a dollar for dollar basis, so long as those expenses were reasonable; for capital invested in the business, however, the company could recover the capital invested *plus* the authorized rate of return. Literally the more it spent, the more it made.[10]

Because the Bell System was the only enterprise providing service to its customers, it was possible to manipulate the pricing of various services to support other agendas – such as universal service. As technology drove the costs of long distance services down, AT&T reduced prices as well – but not as fast as it could have. Instead, with the support of both state and federal regulators, AT&T used the profits from long distance service to subsidize local service rates.[11] With local rates kept at about five dollars a month even into the 1980s, universal service became a reality. The percentage of homes having a telephone increased from fifty to seventy percent between 1945 and 1955, and hit ninety percent in 1969. It drifted slightly higher in the 1970s. When one takes into account those who for whatever reason did not want a telephone, this represented the fulfillment of the mission Theodore

---

10   Money spent on building networks was a capital investment. The costs associated with running the network were expenses. The rate of return was supposed to be equivalent to AT&T's "cost of capital," which was the cost of raising money for the enterprise. As an example, assume simplistically that half of AT&T's money came from debt, costing it four percent, and the other half came from equity, which the experts would say required a ten percent return. AT&T's cost of capital would be seven percent (.5 x .10 plus .5 x .04 = .07).

11   One way this was done was to use what was known as the "Separations Process" to allocate a disproportionate share of costs to the interstate jurisdiction. Separations allocated the capital costs of common plant (i.e., plant used to make both interstate and intrastate calls) to the respective state and federal (or interstate) jurisdictions. As an example, the cost of the copper loops that ran between homes and the central office that served them was split jurisdictionally. The portion of costs allocated to the interstate jurisdiction would be recovered through long distance rates for calls between states; the costs allocated to the intrastate jurisdiction would be recovered either through a combination of long distance rates and local rates. By transferring more costs to the interstate jurisdiction than would have been justified by looking at the relative usage, long distance rates were pushed higher than true economic costs and local rates were kept lower.

Vail had first laid out for the company more than fifty years earlier, without the need of any government subsidies or funding.

Chapter 3

The Invention That Changed the World and the 1956 Decree

The transistor was not only the most important invention of the twentieth century; it also was the most significant invention of the modern era. It ushered in the information age by making more and more powerful computers possible and practical. It literally changed the life of everyone on the planet. The invention was made at AT&T by a team of Bell Labs scientists in 1947, shortly after the end of the Second World War.

The team had been working on an assignment to replace the vacuum tube, the predecessor technology to the transistor. Vacuum tubes rely on the flow of an electrical current through a vacuum, and can be used for amplification, switching or other processing of electronic signals. Such tubes were critical to the development of electronic technology, leading to the growth of radio and television products, sound reproduction, and relevant here, telephone networks whereby signals could be amplified and carried great distances. They also were critical to the development of computers.

Despite the positive attributes of the vacuum tube, it also had its limitations. Vacuum tubes were expensive to make, extremely bulky, and gave off massive quantities of heat. Such attributes made them impractical for low cost, portable devices that we are used to today. The computers of the time were massive, taking up entire rooms. Transistors, on the other hand, could be mass-produced and used only minute amounts of energy, by comparison. AT&T had been looking for technology to improve the cost and performance of the repeaters in its network that amplify sound, allowing telephone calls to be placed in New York, for instance, to be heard in Los Angeles or even London. The transistor met the company's needs perfectly.

AT&T invented the transistor in 1947, and announced it publicly in 1948. The government sued the company in 1949, ostensibly to prevent AT&T from increasing its profitability by "overcharging" the services side of the business for the products bought by it from AT&T's manufacturing arm, Western Electric.[12] If one interprets the purpose of the lawsuit by looking at the relief obtained by the government, however, the case had nothing to do with Western Electric's affiliate pricing. The final decree in the case made no mention, nor did it have any substantive provisions governing the pricing of Western's products. The order instead: (1) required AT&T to license without charge all patents it had received to any entity that wanted them; (2) further required AT&T to license any patents it might receive in the future, essentially without charge, to any entity that wanted them; and (3) restricted AT&T from doing anything other than providing regulated phone service, making the products used in connection with such service, or providing services to the government! With respect to the pricing of Western Electric products, the purported reason for the lawsuit, the 1956 Decree had no restrictions of any kind.

The final judgment in this case was entered by a court in 1956 (the "1956 Decree"), and had the force of law. The massive give-away of

---

12 The services side of AT&T's business had its profits regulated; Western Electric did not. If Western were to sell its products to the service affiliates at "inflated" rates, then not only would it be able to "earn more than it should," but the service side would as well. Remember the services business was entitled to make its authorized rate of return on the capital it invested. If it paid an extra billion dollars a year for its equipment, for instance, and had a ten percent rate or return, the amount of "extra" profits the entire enterprise would reap would be $1.1 billion dollars (an extra billion to Western; and ten percent of the billion for the services side.

AT&T technology was not limited to U.S. companies; it required AT&T to license the technology without charge to anyone, and foreign companies used the AT&T technology as a building block to build their electronics businesses. Sony, for instance came out with the TR-72, a transistor radio containing six transistors that was a huge hit both in Japan and in a number of other markets, including the United States.

AT&T was permitted to charge a "reasonable royalty" with respect to new patents, but the term "reasonable" had a specific meaning attached to it. It was not, as most commonly understood, a reasonable royalty as defined by the value of the patent; rather the term was defined only to permit the recovery of the costs of invention, and here AT&T bore the burden of proof in showing the royalty to be consistent with that standard! As a practical matter, few companies saw the need to obtain licenses even for new patents, since even if AT&T sued them and prevailed, the amounts of money they would owe AT&T for a license would be so small as to make the entire action uneconomic. The result was that virtually all companies felt free to use existing and new technology without permission and without royalties.

Why did the government do something so incredibly irrational as to require the foremost R&D institution in the world, which had just announced the most commercially significant invention of the modern era, to give all of its inventions away for free? The reason, I think, is that the government decided to protect the nascent computer industry, whether at industry behest or on its own, from what it believed was an already-too-powerful AT&T. In 1950, IBM was a substantial company with annual revenues of two hundred sixty-six million dollars, but it was no match for the considerably larger AT&T whose revenues that year were two billion two hundred and twenty-five million dollars. If one looks at the IBM products at the time, one sees how vulnerable IBM was. AT&T invented the transistor in 1947, and an improved "junction transistor" in 1951. IBM introduced the IBM 701 computer in 1952, based solely on vacuum tube technology. New IBM CEO Thomas Watson Jr. issued a policy statement *in 1955* providing that all company products would move to solid-state platforms using transistors by 1959. At the time Watson made the statement, IBM had not secured rights to AT&T's technology. Perhaps IBM lobbied for the result in the decree and knew what was coming, perhaps not. If not, this was a "bet-your-company" policy based on technology that AT&T owned was then not required to give to IBM.

Quite simply, without the transistor, no company could have survived for long in the computer or any other electronics field. It provided an extraordinarily small, inexpensive, and efficient way to manipulate electricity to make things work, so much so that Gordon Moore's prediction (known as Moore's law) that the number of transistors on a single chip will double every two years has been quite accurate in measuring the explosive growth of computing power.

What is even more unfathomable, however, is the 1956 Decree's prohibition on AT&T entering into the computer or other markets itself. One can potentially understand that the government might not want to see AT&T use its inventions to dominate the computer or other electronic industries. But how does one explain the complete prohibition on AT&T using its own technology to compete with IBM or others? Similarly, how does one justify a decision that AT&T not be able to collect even reasonable royalties from those exploiting its inventions?

Stop for a moment and think about the licensing possibilities of the transistor first, and then the other patents such as the digital signal processor and the laser. Because the transistor is the basic building block of all electronics, AT&T had the right for seventeen years to control the markets for electronics and computers. What is a reasonable royalty for IBM, for instance to stay in business? Or Sony? Or Philips? It is fun to play around with licensing strategies in one's mind.

The only certainty is that we're talking about so much money that AT&T royalties would have been, minimally, in the billions of dollars each year.

The decree not only took this possibility away, but it also required AT&T to remain nothing more than a domestic telephone company, a restriction that endured for the next twenty-eight years.[13] The only possible explanation of this added layer of restriction was that the government felt that even after neutralizing the advantages AT&T had earned with its patents, the company still would trounce competitors such as IBM, and the government did not want that to happen.

It is difficult for those of us who witnessed the destruction of the American electronics industry at the hands of more skilled foreign rivals to understand why the government forced AT&T to hand over a treasure-trove of technology, without charge, to any company foreign or domestic that wanted it. True, it was a heady time for the U.S. We were the leading manufacturer, the top inventor, and the top exporter in the world. It was if the Eisenhower administration assumed that foreign competition was not a real possibility, and that their function was to make certain that AT&T didn't get too far ahead of its domestic rivals. AT&T, the 900-pound gorilla, was put in a cage and removed from the fray as foreign companies decimated the rest of the U.S. industry, largely using AT&T inventions to do so.

It wasn't only the transistor that the company was prevented from commercializing, though that would have been enough to control the electronics market. AT&T also invented the high frequency radar (1939); the digital computer (1939); the solar cell (1954); the laser

---

13 The 1956 Decree's so-called "Line of Business' restrictions were lifted by the Modification of Final Judgment," which became effective January 1, 1984.

(1958); satellite transmission of communications signals (1962); the Unix operating system, a machine independent computer language that has become the underlying language of the Internet (1971); fiber optic transmission (1977); digital signal processors (1980); and cellular telephony (1983). AT&T could have held the market for such products or anything using them for the life of the patents (seventeen years), either pursuing the markets themselves or giving licenses to companies it selected. With the 1956 Decree in effect, however, AT&T wasn't permitted even to make back its research costs. Legend has it, for example, that Ken Thompson, the inventor of Unix, would respond to requests for the software by sending the source code on disks, accompanied simply by a note, which read, "Love, Ken."[14]

In 1953, just three years before the government forced AT&T to give away massive amounts of technology to anyone who wanted it, the same Administration executed a married couple, Ethel and Julius Rosenberg, for purportedly giving the Russians the secrets to making an atomic bomb. True, what the Rosenbergs were convicted of giving were military secrets, whereas the forced AT&T giveaway was commercial in nature. The irony, though, is that the government giveaway of AT&T technology did far more lasting damage to this country's interests than the disclosures made by the Rosenbergs.

It is not too much to conclude that the history of the electronics industry in this country would have taken a very different course without the 1956 Decree. No doubt the Decree was intended to keep AT&T out of the computer industry. But it also prevented a well-financed giant from utilizing its patent portfolio to dominate the world of electronics. Rather than finding itself knocked out of one of the most

---

14 Unix has been called "one of the greatest computer operating systems of all times." See Warren Toomy, *The Strange Birth and Long Life of Unix,* IEEE Spectrum (Dec. 2011).

important markets in the coming decades, this country, or at least U.S. companies, could have achieved a truly dominant position.

Why did AT&T agree to the terms of the Decree? The strangest thing of all with respect to the 1956 Decree is that it was considered a major coup for the Company when it was entered. Eisenhower's Attorney General, Herbert Brownell, had reviewed the case shortly after Eisenhower had been sworn in, and had agreed with AT&T to end the case. "AT&T could readily find practices that it would agree to have enjoined *with no real injury to its business*," he is reported to have advised the company. The terms of the agreement were ridiculed in a hearing held by the House antitrust subcommittee, and the deal allegedly had some role in keeping alive rancor towards the company within the Department of Justice, contributing to the decision to sue it again in 1974. It is truly amazing that the terms of the agreement were so poorly understood as to be thought a company victory. The deal was bad for the country and worse for the company, done by people who didn't understand the significance of what they were doing. The 1956 Decree was responsible both for preventing AT&T from capitalizing on its incredible record of invention, and of putting this country's electronics businesses out of business.

Agreeing to the terms of the decree, which forced AT&T to license its patents without compensation, was a mistake so huge that it warrants a description which separates this act from the small, billion dollar mistakes that the company made in the normal course of business. In order to provide some perspective on what were the truly significant errors in judgment by the leaders of AT&T, I have decided to introduce a new term, a "Colossal Mistake," and use it describe errors of, say, one hundred billion dollars or more. The agreement to license the company's patent portfolio without compensation clearly earns the designation as AT&T Colossal Mistake Number One.

Chapter 4

Who Needs the Internet? We've Got PicturePhone!

Not every advance made by a research group is commercially significant. It is the mark of a great company to distinguish between those inventions that should be pursued from those that should not.

Judged by that standard, AT&T was a mind-boggling failure. Time and again it missed market opportunities even when it had invented the technology that made such opportunities possible. It invented but had to play catch-up with cellular telephony, digital switching and fiber transmission, for instance. Technologies it didn't invent had even a lesser chance of being embraced. The most egregious example of this latter marketing miss was something called the Internet. Yes, *the* Internet.

The Internet was pioneered by the United States Department of Defense in the late 1960s. It originated as a packet network[15] used to link computers in different locations together so that computing resources could be shared. The father of the "Arpanet[16]" as it was then called was Larry Roberts, a 29 year old scientist who led the team of engineers that created it. The Arpanet became operational in 1969, originally in four places: UCLA, The University of Utah, the Stanford Research Institute, and the University of California at Santa Barbara.

---

15 Packet networks are data networks that transmit data in chunks or "packets."

16 ARPA stood for the Defense Department's "Advanced Research Projects Agency."

Roberts realized that the same principles used to connect a limited number of locations together could also work on a much larger scale. Recognizing that they would need help, Roberts approached AT&T in 1971. His recollection of what happened is as follows:

"We had decided that it was best if industry ran it, because the government had done its experiment and didn't need to run it anymore. I went to AT&T and made an official offer to them to buy the network from us and take it over. We'd give it to them basically. Let them take it over and they could continue to expand it commercially and sell the service back. So they would have a huge contract [for the government] to buy service back. And they had a huge meeting and they went through Bell Labs and they made a serious decision and they said it was incompatible with their network. They couldn't possibly consider it. It was not something they would use. Or sell."

Why not? The problem was that the company, affecting even many decision makers at Bell Labs, was a "voice" company. Everything AT&T was, everything it was able to do was due to the phenomenal profitability of long distance voice traffic. Yes, AT&T built data networks over the next few decades, and became the leading provider of packet networks. But (and I remember the internal debates) data services couldn't deliver the profits that voice services did. The marketing game plans therefore always were to preserve voice traffic for as long as possible. The idea that voice would simply be an application riding on a data network was anathema to most of the company's leadership.

The various technical improvements to the AT&T network – separate signaling networks that made 800 service and advanced 800 service possible, digital switching, fiber optic transmission – all were advancements to a *voice* network. True, people still wanted to talk to people and voice networks weren't about to disappear overnight. But computers "wanted" to talk to other computers as well, and for this you needed data networks.

What was AT&T working on if it wasn't leading the impending surge in data networking? In 1964, at the World's Fair, AT&T showcased a "PicturePhone" that it had developed after years of effort. People were invited to make video calls between the World's Fair location and booths that had been set up in Disneyland. PicturePhone was the essence of myopia; *it was essentially an effort to build a data application on a voice backbone*! It was a flop commercially --- people didn't buy it because the picture was small, and poor quality, and the equipment itself was bulky and expensive. The company spent another six years working on PicturePhone before rolling it out as a commercial service in 1970 in Pittsburg, Pennsylvania. The company predicted a million customers; at the time it quietly pulled the plug on the service, it had about five hundred.

In retrospect, there are some pretty obvious reasons why the service was such a dismal failure. What AT&T had tried to do was to send broadband signals over the traditional, narrowband voice network. Services offering great picture quality are now commonplace over computers and data networks, which are capable of transmitting huge quantities of data; it was an act of idiotic ingenuity to attempt the same thing over AT&T's voice network, which had no such capabilities.

Today, the Arpanet no longer is known by that name. It grew beyond anyone's expectations and is referred to now as the Internet or the World Wide Web. Whether or not AT&T could have managed its growth as a proprietary network is unclear. But one has to believe that AT&T could have made something of the vast potential of the network for data networking, especially with the U.S. government as its anchor tenant.

How big a mistake was this? I recognize that the analysis here is more speculative! But was it worth a hundred billion dollars to be able to roll out internet service as a branded, proprietary service, with the U.S. government as the anchor tenant? In my view, making that first hundred billion dollars would have been a piece of cake! The decision to reject the government's offer of the fledgling Internet goes down in the books as AT&T Colossal Failure Number Two.

Chapter 5

We Don't Have to; We're the Phone Company

Following the 1956 Decree, AT&T stuck to the telephone business, expanding the reach and capabilities of its network. That same year (1956), AT&T began providing trans-Atlantic service over what it called ""TAT-1," the first trans-Atlantic cable. Prior to this, calls had been carried by radio wave. Cables offered better quality and security. TAT-1 had a capacity for 36 simultaneous calls. AT&T charged $12 for the first three minutes. In 1962, AT&T co-founded Comsat, which it then utilized to launch Telstar, the first communications satellite.[17] It also created a separate signaling network so that services like 800 service became possible.

In 1965, AT&T installed the world's first electronic telephone switch in a local exchange in Succasunna, New Jersey. This promised to vastly reduce the costs of telephone calls by replacing the thousands and thousands of operators who had made the connections for callers previously. About a decade after this, in 1975, AT&T took another giant leap, installing the world's first digital electronic switch, a 4ESS Switch, in Chicago, beginning the computerization of the AT&T network. This switch had the capability to handle 350,000 calls per hour, offering far greater flexibility and speed than the electronic switches it replaced.

---

17 One doesn't normally associate AT&T with rockets. But it was active in the area, and was in fact the prime contractor for the immensely complex anti-ballistic missile system that the country paid to design and develop, but was never implemented due to treaties negotiated between the U.S. and the Soviet Union.

Financially, the company just got stronger and stronger during the 1950's, 60's and 70s. Its assets grew to one hundred fifty five billion dollars by 1983, making it the largest company in the world by far. It had revenues of almost seventy billion dollars, operating income of approximately ten billion dollars, and free cash flow of over seventeen billion dollars *after* spending more than fourteen billion dollars on its construction program. It was also the nation's largest employer, with slightly *more than one million employees.*

The company's incredible power gave life to Lily Tomlin's clever come-dic sketch about an arrogant telephone operator named Ernestine meddling with people's lives, disconnecting them whenever she felt with the words, "We don't have to; we're the phone company." In one sketch involving a Mr. Veedul, she goes through all of his private infor-mation in an effort to make him pay a bill, making the comments along the way that "We are not subject to city, state or federal regula-tion. We're the phone company and we're omnipotent." As he keeps hanging up, she ultimately threatens him with a call from a burley company representative, asking him whether he wouldn't prefer to pay his bill to losing use of his phone, "and possibly one eye."

And yet, there were signs of unrest. Bees are attracted to honey; com-petitors are attracted to areas that are highly profitable. Long distance service must have been as big a lure to competitors as the Spanish treasure ships coming back from the new world were to pirates. A second, lesser but still attractive opportunity was the market for pri-vate switching systems used by corporations, called "private branch exchanges" or PBXs, and other customer premises equipment. AT&T phones lasted and lasted but weren't always what customers wanted. (The joke was that you could have any color phone you wanted -- as long as you wanted black.) And at the high end, AT&T's features were not competitive.

AT&T was not a believer in competition. There was a pervasive belief throughout the company that AT&T did a better job delivering services as a monopoly than those who wanted to come into the market, serve only certain customers, and skim the easy profits. As John Debutts (AT&T CEO from 1972-1979) said, "there is something right about monopoly." Based on this belief, the company filed tariffs at the FCC and the states where it operated, forbidding the attachment to the network of any equipment not provided by AT&T. Under the regulatory frameworks in effect since the 1934 Communications Act, tariffs had the force of law unless found unlawful themselves by the relevant regulatory agency.

AT&T's defense (for this was ultimately challenged both before the FCC and in the courts), was that the restriction against attaching anything not supplied by AT&T to the network was necessary to protect the network from inferior equipment. Perhaps in some small number of cases this was true, but AT&T went well beyond what was defensible or sensible in applying the provision. It sued a maker of clear plastic covers intended to be used as covers for telephone directories, claiming that the directory was part of its network, and the cover was, well, attached to it! It even performed Bell Labs studies of what could happen if the covers obscured telephone numbers printed on the covers, and customers started calling operators instead. In Hush-a-Phone, AT&T opposed the attachment of an acoustic coupler – in other words, a plastic mouthpiece that enabled the speaker to have greater privacy when speaking. AT&T claimed that the attachment could interfere with the clarity of the phone call, and sued its maker! In 1968, the FCC struck down the AT&T tariff provision in the *Carterfone* case, ruling that all customers should be allowed to attach to the network customer-provided equipment that was "privately beneficial without being publicly detrimental."

AT&T was not done being foolish. After Carterphone, AT&T came out with what it called a protective coupling arrangement, or PCA.

Supposedly, it would block injury to the network from faulty customer premises equipment. AT&T filed tariff revisions permitting customers to pick their own customer premises equipment, but requiring in the case of equipment provided by someone other than AT&T that the customer also obtain from AT&T a PCA, which would be placed between the "foreign" equipment and the AT&T network. In most cases, the costs of the PCA made it uneconomic to do anything other than continue renting the AT&T telephone. More than anything else, the PCA led to the dismemberment of the Bell System.

At the high end of the market, the costs of the PCA, while annoying, didn't completely foreclose competitive supply. Litton Industries, a large conglomerate, decided to enter the market to sell private branch exchanges, or PBXs. These were essentially private network switches that a large business would buy in order to provide functionality different than offered by the telephone company.[18] Litton's business failed, however, and it sued AT&T, blaming its lack of business success on the PCA.

AT&T lost a jury trial and hired David Shapiro to look over the shoulders of its existing counsel and see if anything were being missed in preparing an appeal. Dewey Ballentine (a blue blooded Wall Street law firm) had been trial counsel, and Sidley and Austin (a large firm based in Chicago in which Trienens was still a partner) was already looking over their shoulders. I was told to read the entire transcript in order to provide insights to Shapiro who would then share them privately with Howard Trienens.[19]

---

18 For instance, a large customer might want an internal calling network where its employees could call each other using four-digit dialing.

19 Dickstein, Shapiro and Morin had a history with AT&T, having handled a successful antitrust case earlier against AT&T on behalf of a company called Datran. Afterwards, the firm got a steady stream of AT&T business, starting with the Litton case.

While I was convinced that Litton had gone out of business because it just wasn't very good at making and selling PBXs, a disagreement with a finding of fact by a jury wouldn't interest an appellate court. My costly review of every page of the transcript didn't turn up a winning issue on appeal.

Trienens had all of the counsel involved in the case attend a meeting on the executive floor of AT&T headquarters, which at the time was 195 Broadway in New York City. I remember it was winter, because Shapiro – concerned about the weather – wanted us to take the train. A junior partner and I accompanied him. I remember a lot of silly optimism on the part of the Dewey Ballantine lawyers, and I remember being disappointed but not surprised when I later read the appellate decision upholding the jury verdict. The jury had awarded Litton a little more than eighty million dollars, which under the antitrust laws was trebled. Litton made more from that lawsuit than they ever would have made in the PBX business.

The real damage from the lawsuit wasn't the quarter billion dollars AT&T paid in damages to Litton. Rather, it was the fact that AT&T had been found to have acted anti-competitively. That finding carried over and influenced those looking at its behavior in other areas as well. Any time AT&T's behavior was called into question, the subject of its behavior with respect to customer premises equipment was brought up, front and center, to demonstrate the company was at heart a monopolist even where it had no right to be. Every time, AT&T fell into the trap of trying to defend and justify its actions, rather than acknowledging that it had screwed up and moving on from there.

The government sued AT&T in 1974, seeking to split Western Electric from the rest of the company. The basis for the complaint was AT&T's behavior with respect to the interconnection of competitive equipment to the AT&T network, and the PCA. In addition, almost as an after-thought, the government sought the divestiture of Pacific Bell, one of the local companies. The main objective was certainly Western Electric; the FCC had not yet authorized competition in long distance services, so it was difficult to argue that AT&T had acted improperly in limiting it.

Everything changed in 1977. MCI, a competitive upstart, had sought to compete in a limited area of the communications market. MCI didn't seek permission to enter long distance. Rather, it requested authority under Section 214 of the Communications Act to provide point-to-point microwave service for a particular customer.[20] The FCC approved the application, because it would provide a limited amount of competition in the market for private networks, while not raising any of the cross-subsidization issues present in AT&T pricing for long distance services.[21]

The FCC got snookered. No sooner did MCI receive its authorization than it began surreptitiously offering long distance service. It wasn't elegant or of good quality; it used regular business lines to reach an MCI switch, and this then required the customer to enter an authorization code, meaning the customer had to dial extra digits. But it was cheap compared to AT&T pricing, because the latter contained substantial subsidies that enabled AT&T to keep local rates quire low. MCI initially denied it was offering long distance service, so AT&T

---

20   The "M" in MCI, originally stood for "Microwave" as in Microwave Communications, Inc.

21   Private networks are networks that connect a small number of designated locations together. In contrast, the "public switched network" or PSN allows any customer to call any other customer anywhere in the world. Because the subsidies are built into the rates and charges for use of the PSN, a true private line service would not have interfered with the subsidy system. That was what MCI had asked to do, and all the FCC thought it was approving.

put on a demonstration for the FCC, placing long distance calls over the MCI service from the FCC offices in Washington, D.C.

The FCC ordered MCI to cease and desist. MCI refused, finally acknowledging what it was doing, now arguing that the FCC lacked the authority to limit the services it could provide. Legally, the argument is silly, and has never been the law either before or after this case. Judge Skelly Wright, writing on behalf of the three judge panel of the U.S. Court of Appeals for the D.C. Circuit, however, embraced the argument and held that having granted MCI Section 214 authority with respect to the facilities, the FCC could not at some later point limit the services MCI carried on those facilities, even if it found that the public interest required it. Since the FCC had approved the facility without limiting the services, it could not – according to the court – do so now.

Judge Wright likely thought he was striking a blow for competition. Put that to one side for a moment and evaluate his decision on the legal merits, and it is clear that the case was incorrectly decided. The same court had ruled in an earlier case that AT&T did in fact have to obtain authority under Section 214 of the Communications Act (the same provision being interpreted in the MCI case) in order to offer channel services to cable companies.[22] Nor is the MCI decision followed today. Shortly before I left AT&T in August 2004, we had decided to cease providing 900 service, and we were forced by the FCC to go through a Section 214 proceeding. This was purely a case of withdrawing a ser-

---

22 The relevant text of the statute, adopted in 1934, reads: "No carrier shall undertake the construction of a new line... *or shall acquire or operate any line or shall engage in transmission over or by means of such line* ...unless and until there shall have been obtained from the Commission [a certificate of convenience and necessity]... (emphasis added). The italicized words give the Commission authority over services. This is clear because the language referring to "construction of a new line" is separated by the word "or" before the language of "transmission over...such line," appears.

vice; we were not planning nor did we ask to withdraw any facilities from service.

If one thinks through the sort of proceeding the FCC would have had to have to keep all regulatory options open, one sees how unworkable Judge Wright's analysis was. According to his ruling, the FCC would have had to have full hearings on every single service that MCI could have offered using the facilities in question, whether or not MCI intended to offer them now or in the future. Opponents of the use of facilities for any possible service would have had to intervene. Simple licensing decisions could have dragged on for months or years; something like MCI's application would have taken years or even decades.

The absolute mess this would create at the agency level would become much worse if one of the parties appealed. Appeals from FCC decisions normally are to the United States Courts of Appeal. These are "Title III" Courts, which means that they are limited to hearing "cases or controversies" by Article 3 of the United States Constitution. Hypothetical disputes are not considered cases or controversies. A decision by the FCC concerning a service that *could* be offered over certain facilities but which the builder of the facilities had no plans to offer, would almost certainly be viewed as a hypothetical question the federal appeals court could not review. In other words, the impact of Judge Wright's bizarre interpretation would have been to swamp the FCC in endless and pointless proceedings, which then would not have been reviewable. Congress could not have intended such a result!

The sort of nightmarish proceeding that would be required to implement Section 214 as interpreted in that decision is not necessary for the simple reason that the decision was just plain wrong. A service like MCI offered is plainly a "transmission over such lines," and as such, the FCC obviously had authority over the offering of services independent from the construction of facilities. There is nothing in the statute to support Judge Wright's logic, and the FCC has in other cases ruled on discrete services under the statute, with the support of the same court.

Still, the decision by the court was the law and had to be implemented. (Review by the Supreme Court is discretionary with that Court in most instances, and the Court for reasons it didn't explain chose not to review this case.) MCI began offering long distance service, while paying nothing for the connections to AT&T's network, and nothing towards the costs of local service. AT&T's rates, in contrast, included substantial subsidies that had grown over time so that local rates could remain low.

There were two possible responses to competitive entry under such circumstances: first, AT&T could have accepted the inevitability of sound economics prevailing over time, and could have sought to eliminate the internal cross-subsidies between its services. This would have meant, of course, that local rates would have had to be increased – perhaps to levels two or three times what they were at the time. There would be intense opposition to such a rebalancing of rates from the public; and it was anathema to the state regulators who would have to approve such rate increases. Approving a local rate increase was political dynamite; it was the one action that could jeopardize the jobs of the members of the public service commission.

Moreover, the regulatory rules that caused an over-allocation of costs to interstate long distance services were difficult to change, and impossible to change quickly. Congress had mandated that any changes in the formulae governing the allocation of costs had to be the subject of hearings before something called "the state-federal joint board," comprised of members of the FCC and state commissions. This board would hold round after round of hearings, all conducted through paper submissions. Its decision, when finally issued, was advisory only;

final decision-making authority rested with the FCC. But if the FCC wanted to duck a tough issue, or if it really needed facts that hadn't been developed the first round, it would remand the proceeding back to the Joint Board, who would start over again. In other words, anything that had to come before the Board would take years before a final decision would be implemented.

In short, the path to create a rational economic structure based on costs was long, and not very clear. Add to that the difficult task of educating the public about the need to raise local rates and the option became completely unattractive.

The second option was to impose on any new entrants the same artificial charge AT&T was making as a contribution to local service. This could be done very quickly simply by introducing the charge in a tariff filing, and had the added virtue from AT&T's point of view of imposing a rate so high that it likely would put the would-be competitors out of business. AT&T chose this course, filing the ENFIA, or Exchange Network Facilities for Interstate Access, tariff. The Commission suspended the tariff, and began an investigation in 1978 of what the compensation should be. That proceeding and the first "access charges" were finalized by the Commission on January 1, 1984, the first day of the break-up of AT&T.[23] For reasons never made clear to me, AT&T decided to turn over the handling of the ENFIA proceeding to Dickstein, Shapiro and Morin, and David Shapiro gave the project to me. At the time, I knew nothing of the underlying issues, nor of the terrible significance that the interconnection payments would assume. I therefore listened to the AT&T strategists who thought that making

---

23 The tariff proceeding was CC docket No. 78-371. The FCC at the same time issued a rulemaking to establish the appropriate access charges for interstate long distance service, CC Docket No. 78-72. When I joined AT&T in mid-1983, I was given the responsibility for handling the rulemaking as well.

the charges as high as possible was a good thing, and helped create the monster that eventually destroyed the company.

It was a classic case of fighting the last war...

Chapter 6

Working in the Belly of the Beast

I began working at AT&T on July 1, 1983, and immediately plunged into the access issue – our comments on how the FCC should restructure the long distance market were due soon, and I was given the responsibility of drafting the "Bell System" position. It didn't strike me as odd that I as a newcomer was handling such an important proceeding. For one thing, I had been handling it as outside counsel. Also, most of the experienced lawyers were working feverishly on the "Plan of Reorganization," the master plan to split the company into eight companies, effective January 1, 1984.

This truly was a gigantic task. People and assets had to be split into groupings that worked. For instance, seven new Chief Executive Officers had to be picked, as well as the supporting staffs. Every single organization was involved. Contracts with third parties had to be reviewed so that the rights and obligations would be clearly assigned to AT&T or one of the newly formed companies. Most important, the network would have to be disassembled with the seven local companies taking the local assets, and AT&T taking the assets primarily associated with long distance services, while ensuring that it still functioned as before.

During my first week of work, I was trying to sort through some of the comments made by various officers on my first draft when a man walked into my office and introduced himself as my boss, and gave me directions as to what he wanted to be included in the next draft. He also told me that he wanted to see the next draft before I showed it to anyone else, shaving two days off the time I had to complete it. Panicked, I went to see the "Sixth" level officer who had hired me, and who had assured me at the time that I would work directly for her. I told her, with some agitation I had just learned that I was a "fourth level," reporting to a "fifth" level who in turn reported to her.

She didn't miss a beat. She explained that I would of course come to her directly on all substantive matters, explaining that is what she had meant all along. She had made one other statement during the hiring process that if not plain untrue, was overly optimistic: she had said that the company headquarters would be moving from 195 Broadway in Manhattan to bucolic Basking Ridge, New Jersey in a few months, and I should buy a house convenient to Basking Ridge. I did, and commuted the two and one half hours each way to 195 Broadway for the next year and a half.

My son, who was in part responsible for my being at AT&T, was fully responsible for my sleep deprivation during the period when I wrote the pleadings setting forth AT&T's positions on interconnection. Between his waking up and my need to get up at 4:30 to catch an early train so that I could get to work at a reasonable hour, I didn't sleep much. Fortunately, the company had a policy that anyone working past 9 p.m. was entitled to take a limo home. During the first few months when the pressure of getting our comments and reply comments together was in full swing, it was something I did virtually every night.

My immediate supervisor turned out to be something of an odd duck. He was a bachelor in his late forties, and wore hairpieces. I would never have noticed, but (so the more observant secretaries told me) he had in fact two hair pieces: one that made it look like he needed a haircut and a second one that made it look like he had just gotten his hair cut. In the next few years as the company lurched towards becoming a competitive entity, more than half of the attorneys were laid off; he was one who didn't make the cut. He was like a lot of other people caught in the fundamental change hitting the company: he was a very nice man with a good sense of humor, but with average skills. In the maelstrom that the company faced, that was deemed insufficient.

For the first six months I was at AT&T (July 1 – December 31, 1983), we also circulated our pleadings to representatives of the local Bell companies. At the time, there was no sense that we would be at each other's throats in a few years. As John Zeglis later explained to me, he (who was by then the General Counsel) had a choice: either he had to permit the Bell companies though they did not yet formally exist to represent themselves at the FCC, or if he didn't want that, we had a fiduciary duty to represent their interests. He chose the latter, believing that in this way we could present a balanced view. In fact, what we espoused at the time eventually helped destroy AT&T.

There were two key issues in dispute: (1) first, what should be the level of access charges paid by long distance companies to local companies for the use of the local plant to originate and terminate interstate calls? and (2) should all long distance companies pay the same or should MCI, Sprint and others get a discount reflecting the fact that their access arrangements were of lesser quality?

AT&T had been fighting since 1977 to have the charges paid by our long distance competitors based on the historical Bell System practices rather than costs, and we continued that stance here. After all, the local Bell companies that would be enriched were our sister companies and would be legally precluded from competing with us by the Modification of Final Judgment, which would take effect the same day as the access tariffs. And our internal strategists were convinced that the new competitors, being thinly capitalized, would not survive if they had to pay anything close to equivalent contributions towards the costs of local service.

The FCC, however, couldn't let competition disappear. The Bell System break-up was extremely unpopular with most of the country, and the usual public deference that someone in government must know what they are doing was absent. The popular sentiments of the time were captured in a sign employees put up at a number of AT&T locations. It read:

"There are two giant entities in this country, and they both have an amazing influence on our daily lives…One has given us radar, sonar, stereo, teletype, the transistor, hearing aids, the artificial larynx, talking movies, and the telephone. The other has given us the Civil War, the Spanish American War, the First World War, the Second World War, the Korean War, the Vietnam War, double-digit inflation, double-digit unemployment, the Great Depression, the Gasoline Crisis, and the Watergate Fiasco. Guess which one is now telling the other how to run its business?"

For the MFJ to work, there had to be competitors. MCI, Sprint and a host of other companies therefore made the predictable arguments, claiming that if they had to pay access charges they would go out of business. And, they pointed out, they received inferior access arrangements to those given to AT&T. AT&T's customers dialed "1," the area code and the number. The other carriers' customers had to dial extra digits as an authorization code. Unlike the story on the equipment side, however, the inferior arrangements were a consequence of how the network had been engineered in a monopoly environment and how "Other Common Carriers" such as MCI (collectively referred to as "OCCs") had first entered the business, not because of any anticompetitive intent.

The AT&T network was hierarchical. There were hundreds and hundreds of "Class 5" central offices spread out serving local communities. When a person in a local calling area calls another person in the same local calling area, it would not be a toll call for which long distance charges would apply. The local switch would simply transfer the call to the line of the called party. Where, however, a call was placed to someone outside of the local calling area, the switch transferred the call to a trunk carrying traffic between the class 5 local central office and the class 4 toll office. The class 4 office would do the necessary translations to the numbers and send the call to the local office that served the called customer. The network was engineered with a single trunk going to a single long distance company (AT&T) because AT&T was the only game in town at the time it engineered its network. "Choice" of toll carriers wasn't important from an engineering point of view because it didn't exist in reality.

When MCI entered the long distance market, it didn't say it wanted to provide long distance service so please re-engineer the network and build us some trunks.

It entered surreptitiously by ordering regular business lines, and hauling the calls to a switch of its own. It was an awkward arrangement, but one of MCI's own making. Nevertheless, once what it was doing was public knowledge, MCI began complaining that AT&T was giving it second-rate connections, insisting that it was part of a plot designed to put it out of business. It fought against paying access charges at all, but demanded huge discounts from the access charges AT&T was going to pay, at the very least, claiming that such discounts were necessary to allow it to compete against the superior quality of the AT&T network arrangements.

The FCC's first order established an extremely large access charge — more than ten cents a minute per end, or twenty cents a conversation minute, and set an OCC discount at 35%. Subsequent orders revised the charge down and the discount up, as the OCCs launched a ferocious lobbying campaign, with a single message: we will go out of business with only a 35% discount. The second order produced a discount of 45%, and the third order moved it to 55%. If it was going to err, the FCC wanted to err on the side of the OCCs. If they went out of business now, when the Bell System was being broken up so that they could compete, it would be a major embarrassment for government policy.

There is little question that if the OCCs had needed a 90% percent discount in order to compete, the FCC would have ordered it. The government had made a big bet on competition in telecom, and was willing to take as much money out of AT&T's hide as necessary to make it work.

Chapter 7

The Modification of Final Judgment and the Break-Up of AT&T

In 1974, only months after President Nixon resigned and President Ford became president, the government sued AT&T once again. As in the 1949 case that resulted in the 1956 Decree, the principal focus of the case was on Western Electric and the anticompetitive actions (described above in connection with the Litton lawsuit) that AT&T allegedly used to injure would-be competitors. In other words, the government claimed AT&T had used its monopoly power in services to injure competitors seeking to compete with it for equipment sales. This time, however, the government asked as part of the relief it was seeking that the court require AT&T to divest one of the operating telephone companies. Once again, AT&T resisted settling the case (which it could have done) on terms that required only the divestiture of its equipment business.

The problem was, in two words, Bell Labs. Most of the inventions made by the Labs were incorporated into equipment made by Western Electric. If Western were to be divested, it would have been exceedingly difficult to argue for retention of the Labs. Moreover, Western paid almost the entire bill for the Labs, which would have made life far more complicated if the two were separated.[24] The leadership of AT&T was enamored with the Labs, as was the country. No one wanted to

---

24   Funding for the specific projects done by the Labs was from the business unit requesting the work be done. The basic research bill was allocated to the units on the basis of proportionate revenues.

leave a legacy that they were the person(s) who had given away Bell Labs.

Major antitrust cases are slow moving and take political lifetimes to run their course. After Ford came Carter, and after Carter came Reagan. With the Republican Reagan in office, AT&T decided to make an all out effort to kill the case through political channels.

Most of the Reagan Administration was opposed to the Department of Justice's plan to break up the company. AT&T's Chairman Charlie Brown and General Counsel Howard Trienens were active behind the scenes, and had strong allies in Caspar Weinberger, the Secretary of Defense, who believed strongly that fragmenting the AT&T network would jeopardize national security, and Malcolm Baldridge, the Secretary of Commerce, who believed the country needed a strong AT&T in the equipment market to fight off the increasingly aggressive Asian competitors. On the other hand, William Baxter, the Assistant Attorney General in charge of the Department of Justice's Antitrust Division, believed in the case, and fought vigorously to avoid having it dismissed. The dispute came to a head in a cabinet meeting, where Weinberger and Baldridge sought to have Reagan order the case to be dismissed. After the arguing was over, Reagan told a folksy story about postage rates going up while phone rates went down, without indicating the point of his story. That was it. Reagan with all of his faculties almost certainly would have killed the case, but he was human and frail. Reagan failed to grasp the issues or act decisively in the face of disagreement among those he trusted. A case in motion tends to stay in motion; Reagan never did express his views of whether he felt that was good or bad.

AT&T also was unlucky with respect to the federal district court judge assigned to hear the case. His name was Harold Greene and he was a dogged jurist, one who was determined to see the case proceed to conclusion. He also thought that AT&T had gotten an unduly favorable settlement of the earlier lawsuit with the 1956 Decree, and was determined not to let it happen again. Greene totally missed the real impact of the 1956 Decree, looking instead solely at AT&T's existing telephone operations. It is true but besides the point that the telephone operations were not affected by the decree.

Having failed to accomplish its goal in the Executive branch, AT&T next tried in Congress. AT&T mounted a furious lobbying campaign in Congress to implement a bill that would have sanctioned the activity being challenged. It gained sufficient momentum that the Justice Department at one point proposed that the court case be delayed for nine months to see whether the bill would become law. Judge Greene rejected the notion of any such delay, and forced the government to finish putting on its case.

It is unclear whether AT&T's disastrous defense of the government case was due more to the misfortune of having Judge Greene as the finder of fact, or its own numerous missteps. Howard Trienens picked George Saunders, one of his partners at Sidley & Austin, to try the case. No doubt Saunders was brilliant but he didn't have the personality that would have enabled him, as Shapiro had recommended, to find some way to convince the jury (or in this case the judge) that they had things in common. I met Saunders only once when he visited our firm to "help" with the ENFIA proceeding. He lectured me on things he didn't understand nearly as well as I did. When I made the point that we had no evidence in the record that local rates were in fact below cost and required a subsidy, he disagreed. Going up to the blackboard we had been using, he scribbled with great emphasis SPF = 3.3 (SLU).

That was the formula for the allocation of common plant costs to the state and federal jurisdictions. It provided that the interstate jurisdiction would be assigned 3.3 times the allocation that would have resulted from a straight allocation based on relative usage. That alone proved nothing, a fact that he clearly didn't understand. (If the cost of providing local service was in fact $4/month, then a $5 rate required no further subsidy. We had no evidence in the record of what local service costs were, so our position that local service rates were below cost was mere assertion.) My reaction to the meeting was, "God, what an arrogant man!" He seemed to have that effect on many who he met. Given that AT&T's challenge was to convince the judge that the company hadn't acted heavy-handed, I can't imagine a worse choice.

AT&T defended its actions through the government's presentation of its direct case. Before presenting its defense, however, AT&T made a motion to dismiss, a customary tactic, seeking dismissal on the grounds that the government's case was legally insufficient to prove a violation of the anti-trust laws. AT&T was set back on its heels by Judge Greene, who wrote a careful, meticulous and totally hostile decision, denying AT&T's motion. Finding that the government had proven its case, the judge left little doubt that the defensive arguments the company had already outlined at the beginning of trial would be unavailing.

AT&T therefore entered into settlement discussions with the Department of Justice. If you believe that removal of the line of business restrictions would result in great AT&T successes in new markets such as the computer market, then you would believe that the initial settlement negotiated by AT&T was quite shrewd. The settlement split the company imperfectly between those operations that were competitive (long distance and the equipment markets) and those that would remain monopolies without competition (local service). AT&T would keep Long Lines (i.e., its long distance business), Western Electric and Bell Labs. AT&T's twenty-two local entities would be organized into seven companies, referred to as the Regional Bell Operating Companies, or RBOCs.

The Modification of Final Judgment, or MFJ[25], as the settlement was called, also came up with a new term, "Local Access and Transport Area" or LATA to define the boundaries within which the RBOCs could offer service. Theses areas were larger than local exchanges, but still small enough to leave the bulk of the long distance (or interLATA) market to the long distance companies like AT&T and MCI. The MFJ prohibited the RBOCs from offering interLATA services or from making or selling equipment. AT&T would be relieved of the patent licensing requirements and the line of business restrictions of the 1956 Decree.

The reason why so much attention was paid to giving the RBOCs larger service areas (LATAs rather than local exchanges) and to putting the Bell System operating entities into a smaller number of Regional Companies was because Judge Greene was concerned about the financial viability of the RBOCs. After all, the RBOCs themselves and their allies were all predicting that the RBOCs would be too poor to survive in the harsh world they were about to enter.

The RBOCs wanted to increase the size of the LATAs to increase their share of the long distance market. Judge Greene, motivated by his concerns over their health, agreed on condition that the RBOCs sign a commitment to allow intraLATA competition from the long distance companies, *except where prohibited by state law.* The deal was struck, and before the ink was dry, the RBOCs started an intense lobbying campaign, universally successful, to have the state public service commissions or state legislatures declare the provision of intraLATA services by anyone but the RBOCs to be unlawful!

---

25 Due to some early procedural skirmishing, the settlement was structured as a modification of the 1956 Decree, as opposed to a new proceeding.

A settlement of an antitrust case between the Department of Justice and a company is not like a settlement of private litigation where the parties may agree to anything they want and the judge plays no role. Here, the Tunney Act required the judge to review the settlement to determine whether it was in the public interest. Judge Greene threw the proceeding open, allowing anyone and everyone to submit comments as to whether the settlement was in the public interest, and the feeding frenzy began. NARUC, an association of state regulatory commissioners, argued that the seven divested local companies were going to have to raise local rates, because they wouldn't otherwise be able to survive. Both Judge Greene and the Department of Justice were adamant that the case not be perceived as causing local rates to go up. After all, competition is supposed to produce lower rates, and here all these experts were saying that the rates would have to go up from what the old monopolist charged!

This concern prompted Judge Green to condition his approval of the settlement on the highly profitable Yellow Pages directory business being taken from AT&T and given to the regional companies. There was no allegation of any wrongdoing related to the Yellow Pages business; the whole reason for its transfer was the concern about the regional companies financial health and the possibility of local rate increases. The Yellow pages business at the time was the highest margin business within the Bell System, making about three hundred million dollars annually in profits, coincidentally about what AT&T had been spending on basic research each year within Bell Labs.

It is a testament to the regional companies' avarice, shamelessness, and lobbying skills that once they got the Yellow Pages business, they were successful in getting it deregulated in state after state. That meant that Yellow Pages profits could not be considered or used to support local rates, which could (and did) rise independent of the Yellow Pages business. As for the Yellow Page profits, those were kept by the RBOCs and used by them for whatever purpose they wanted.

Like the Yellow Pages, the cellular licenses held by AT&T were not the subject of any charges of wrong-doing. These also were competitive services; the FCC had awarded a minimum of two licenses for every market. But the RBOCs wanted the licenses not on the basis of some principled argument but because they saw great value in, as well as a future competitive threat from, wireless services. They argued that the service was more like local service. The argument was specious, and AT&T should have ended up with the licenses. The only problem, and it was a huge problem, was that AT&T didn't want the licenses enough to fight for them!

AT&T had invented cellular service. (Motorola had made the first cell phone, but the service design itself was a creation of Bell Labs.) When it was considering whether to enter the market to build cellular telephones, AT&T did something it considered prudent yet in retrospect was incredibly stupid: it hired McKinsey & Co., high-priced management consultants, to size the opportunity before AT&T entered the market for cell phones. In other words, it assumed without basis that McKinsey would understand telecom markets better than its own people. McKinsey advised AT&T that the opportunity was negligible. The power requirements of cell phones were substantial. Based on the battery technology *at the time,* a person would have to lug around a prohibitively heavy battery. The most reasonable view, McKinsey advised, was that one might have such phones in cars, but even then they likely would be toys that only the very rich could afford. (The high prices were based on high development costs divided by a limited number of phones.)

McKinsey sized the entire market demand at a few hundred thousand users. Add to this pessimistic and hopelessly inaccurate view of the wireless future the fact that the wireless licenses would require the holder to invest substantial amounts of capital to build out the new systems, and the market didn't seem that attractive. (Unless the license holder invested substantial amounts of money to build wireless networks, the FCC could and likely would take the license back.) Consequently, AT&T chose not to fight for the licenses. Charlie Brown, the AT&T Chairman unfortunately was influenced by McKinsey and made the decision to give the wireless licenses to the RBOCs. No compensation was paid. Of all the blunders made by AT&T, this one was by far the largest: the number of mobile phones sold to date is not a few hundred thousand, but 1.6 *billion*. (I recognize that this number, reached in early 2012, will seem trivial in a few more years -- it is the fastest growing part of the telecom business!) The size of the wireless services business in the United States is between $250 and 300 billion dollars annually now, not a bad little business.

AT&T's choice to pursue a wired future is filled with irony. AT&T made the same mistake Western Union made decades earlier when that company had chosen to stick with the old technology and let others invest in the new. Despite the fact that the wireless licenses were, in retrospect, the single most valuable asset owned by AT&T, they were given to the RBOCs without a fight and without a dime of compensation!

Change this single decision and you would still have a healthy, wealthy AT&T. While it would have had competition in the wireless business, it had the most complete set of licenses, access to capital and a name that meant something to customers. (Even before AT&T entered the cellular services market, it had done customer surveys to determine the company customers believed offered the best wireless service: the answer was AT&T!!). To be the number one provider in a fast growing market, a market with high barriers to entry and good margins, is not all bad.

The decision to give the wireless licenses away to the RBOCs goes down as AT&T Colossal Failure Number Three.

Chapter 8

So This is the Computer Business?

The 1984 Modification of Final Judgment lifted the line of business restrictions (imposed by the 1956 Decree) that had prevented AT&T for 28 years from entering the computer business. AT&T's 1984 annual report was all exuberance and optimism, talking about the convergence of the computing and telecommunications markets into the "Information" market. It sounded good, and had been made up by AT&T's public relations department, but it didn't reflect reality. Companies still bought mainframes, and both companies and individuals bought desk computers and laptops. Whatever words AT&T wanted to use were fine, but did it have the products?

Moore's Law, holding that the number of transistors that can fit on a single chip will double every two years, remarkably, has held true thus far. What it means practically is that the computer industry moves very rapidly, and that a machine that is powerful now will seem obsolete in a year or two. Into this fast-paced maelstrom, the slow-moving, even ponderous AT&T plunged, hoping rather than planning for the best. It formed a new unit of the company, AT&T Data Systems, and prepared to take on all comers in the computer market.

AT&T decided to partner with an Italian company to make laptop computers for the low end of the market. AT&T gave Olivetti complete control of the design and manufacture of its IBM-compatible PCs for a nine-year period. The deal was exclusive meaning that AT&T committed to buy such computers only from Olivetti. The problem with this arrangement was that Olivetti couldn't keep up with the market.

Soon after AT&T introduced its first machine, it found itself trailing the market in both price and function. Yet, it couldn't terminate the deal or buy from other sources. It wasn't as if this was a minor deal that flew by under the radar screen; this was the big-time, and the deal was as bone-headed as one can possibly imagine!

Separately, AT&T had another company build Unix-based PCs for it; these wouldn't sell either. People are finicky, and didn't want to buy computers for which little application software existed, and which were not compatible with anything else then available. Though Unix was an excellent software language, it had languished while the majority of users bought PCs based on Microsoft MS-DOS. Third party software developers, therefore, generally wrote their applications for computers that used MS-DOS, not Unix. Machines using MS-DOS were called "IBM-compatible" because of IBM's early lead in this market. AT&T's entry in the IBM-compatible market was the machine build by Olivetti.

AT&T was not ready to give up. It kept looking for a major player to buy. Finally, it decided on NCR, the cash register and automatic teller machine ("ATM") company.[26] NCR had great aspirations, and had developed a massively parallel computer that was alleged to be faster than IBM's fastest mainframes. NCR, however, didn't want to be bought. Finally, after discussions went nowhere, AT&T launched a hostile tender offer to buy the company. AT&T's offer was sufficiently generous to win the day. AT&T now owned NCR for a mere $7.4 billion dollars.

In between the mainframes and the PCs is a respectably large mid-range market segment for computers, a market that AT&T tried to

---

26 Like many other companies, NCR had changed its name to be its initials. It was originally known as the National Cash Register Company.

address with an adaptation of the 3B processors. These processors had been developed by Bell Labs to be the brains of AT&T's telecom switches. The 3Bs were fine machines, perhaps too fine. They had been designed to have zero down-time, and for customers wanting computers for tasks less demanding than running telephone networks, they were overkill.

Computing speed is necessary, but not sufficient. More important are the applications that enable companies to do something with all that processing power. This was IBM's strength, and AT&T's weakness. AT&T never made a real dent against market leaders IBM and Digital Equipment Corp. Finding itself stymied at the low end, embarrassed at the high end, and unable to sell its machines in the middle, AT&T lost literally billions in its ill-conceived entry into the computer market. If one looks carefully at what AT&T did to support its entry into computers, it is clear that it didn't have a clue about what it was doing. Both tactics and strategy were either totally missing or not executed. It was a case of gross human error.

Yet there was no accountability. The Board didn't fire (or even chastise) anyone[27], nor did CEO Bob Allen in turn do anything about the executives who led the computer debacle. To the contrary, one of them – Rich McGinn – was about to get a very plum assignment as the Chief Executive Officer of Lucent. Perhaps the AT&T Board saw some gem of brilliance in his computer tour that I have failed to grasp...

Nah!!

---

27   It was Allen's predecessor, James Olson, who bought NCR.

Chapter 9

Atlanta Interlude – Time in the Trenches

In 1985, I moved to Atlanta in order to get a promotion. There was an opening for a General Attorney, a "fifth level" job. The person who had held that job had joined an outside law firm, hoping AT&T would then have little choice but to use him at several hundred dollars an hour as opposed to an internal salary. The mission of the regional legal teams by that time was to get AT&T deregulated in the states, seek access reductions from the RBOCs, and otherwise participate in whatever proceedings would pop up from time to time. Upon my arrival in Atlanta, I was given responsibility for the Southern Bell states – North and South Carolina, Georgia and Florida. I had attorneys who did North Carolina and Georgia with little help from me; I spent my time in Florida and South Carolina. State regulatory proceedings were similar to FCC proceedings with one big difference: whereas the FCC proceedings were exclusively paper proceedings, the states still had oral arguments, with live witnesses.

In the eighties, the FCC viewed it as a big part of its job to prevent AT&T from harming competitors. One such effort was the Computer II inquiry. The FCC imposed rules to ensure AT&T didn't use its power as a services provider to skew the market for equipment. AT&T was required to have separate sales forces, for instance. In other words, the same person couldn't sell you services and a PBX. Inefficient? Sure it was, but the Bell System had earned some level of oversight with its behavior in this area.

As a result of overly conservative legal advice from AT&T lawyers, however, AT&T first went much farther than was required. It essentially split the entire company into two entities, putting all the people working on services in one entity, and those working on equipment in another. One day, someone woke up, realized that level of separation wasn't required after all, and the company then decided to put the pieces back together under the sexy moniker "the End User Organization."

What a clash of cultures! The upper-level lawyers in the region who supported the equipment business had been in the regions for a long time. Their existence had been, and still was, somewhat sleepy. The services personnel were almost all new, because the former Bell System personnel in the regions had more often than not gone to the RBOCs. Those of us on the services side tended to be younger, more aggressive, and more bullheaded.

I worked for an absolutely delightful man, Patrick Walsh, who was an Irish storyteller without equal. He asked me to attend a meeting he was going to have with the head lawyer for the equipment side shortly after I transferred to Atlanta, the purpose of which was to tell the previously independent equipment-side lawyers that they now worked for Walsh. We had a brief lunch, with the usual chit-chat for a minute or so. Then the equipment lawyer asked, without any attempt to lower his voice, "So tell me Pat, you got any Jews?"

I wished I had been clever enough to respond, "Go fish. You got any rednecks?" But I was too surprised to do anything other than say, "Yeah. I'm a Jew."

He didn't seem embarrassed in the least. His next question was, "So what kind of Jew are you?"

"I'm a nuthin' Jew," I said, intending that to be the last word of that conversation. It was. It wasn't until later that I discovered that his question wasn't motivated by bigotry as much as it was a desire to compare notes about these strange creatures. He had recently hired two Jewish attorneys who didn't get along with each other. That is probably why he had asked which type of Jew I was!

The first year and a half I was with AT&T, I had been at headquarters insulated from the real world, writing pleadings. Now I was in the region. I would have gone crazy without Walsh. The two of us would to go for private lunches where we talked about work and life. We wouldn't exclude anyone. We simply announced that we were going to go have sushi, asking if anyone else wanted to go. Sushi was viewed at the time by most of our colleagues as pretty disgusting, and the invitation to go eat "raw fish" guaranteed that we would dine alone.

There were plenty of wonderful people there. My secretary, Salil, was a gem. The first year I was in the region, I wrote a brief seeking "deregulation" of AT&T's operations in Florida, packing every bit of evidence I could gather up in a monster brief with over a hundred footnotes. (These were the days as I recall where word processing was still somewhat primitive, and dealing with that number of footnotes would have been a sufficient defense to homicide.) Despite my refusal to simplify the brief, she completed it, including making the obligatory (but ultimately unimportant) last minute changes.

At the time, we were a fully regulated utility – we had to keep our books so that the Commissions in the various states could determine that we didn't make too much money, and all services had to be filed in tariffs. Our competitors (MCI, Sprint and other smaller carriers) were not regulated and could do whatever they wanted. For example, AT&T was in a fierce competitive war with MCI during this period. MCI could roll out a new price plan, advertise it and make it immediately effective. We could not. Each state had its own notice periods governing how long AT&T must wait following the filing of a tariff before the rates became effective. Most were thirty days; some longer. In order to roll out a national pricing plan, we had to file and then wait for the longest applicable waiting period. We thought it was very unfair. In any event, my brief with all of its footnotes failed to get AT&T deregulated.

The following year, I filed a five page brief, asserting we should be deregulated because we no longer had market power, with no evidence of any kind. We won. Go figure.

For whatever reason, the people in the region seemed more down to earth and more fun than the people at headquarters. I thoroughly enjoyed my time with them. Among those I spent the most time with were Gene Coker, a consummate southern gentleman; Bob "Bubba" McKee, a Yankee from Philadelphia and the office prankster and humorist; and Mike Tye, a shrewd lawyer and lobbyist with an accent so-o-o-o southern that you could have counted from one to one hundred before he finished saying my name "Dan," making two very long syllables out of it! (Sort of like "Dayyyyyyyyyyy – yunnnnnnn.")

Working in the region was eye opening in a number of ways. I quickly came to the conclusion that we could not afford my predecessor's legal bills as outside counsel. Florida was an active state and he was not embarrassed to rake us over the financial coals in doing what he used to do as inside counsel. I fired him, and began commuting to Tallahassee on a regular basis to handle proceedings before the Public Utilities Commission myself. Fortunately for me, I had received my undergraduate degree from the University of Florida, and that was enough to gain some credibility with the Commission that I wasn't just some damned Yankee come to make trouble.

Most of the commissions were happy enough to deregulate AT&T. But all of them were smarting over the divestiture because they now had us fighting with Southern Bell about access charges, and they hated that. Many Commissioners had taken the jobs as political pay-offs for past favors, and didn't relish having to make hard decisions.. I remember in particular a case in South Carolina, where I was cross-examining fairly hard the Southern Bell cost witness, to the point that he began losing his composure. I made the mistake of looking at the Commissioners to make certain they were getting it. One was listening and looked distinctively uncomfortable; two were sleeping; and two had left shortly before the fireworks began. It was life in the slow lane.

I don't mean to suggest that we got treatment equal to that the RBOCs got from the State PUCs. We didn't; they routinely clobbered us! The top lobbyists from the Bell System days overwhelmingly went to the RBOCs and it was clear that they enjoyed a "home field" advantage. Time and again, the RBOCs were able to work their wills on the PUCs. The Commissioners did hate to see us fighting, but that didn't change the end result—which was that the RBOCs almost always won.

Sometimes the Commissions' animosity to the divestiture bubbled over. In Florida, for example, a hostile Commission insisted that AT&T pay a "divestiture surcharge" in the tens of millions of dollars to Southern Bell to compensate that company for its costs of dealing with the divestiture, a ruling upheld by the Florida Supreme Court. In all the hysteria, no one really looked at the local companies' earnings, which began to skyrocket due to (1) the high level of access charges; (2) other money thrown at them (such as Yellow Pages profits) to avoid the need for local rate increases; and (3) the local rate increases that the Bells began pushing through nonetheless. It was a grand fleecing of the public, blamed on AT&T, but in fact the culprits were the local companies!!

Do the math: the total amounts paid by consumers were going up, whereas the share of the revenues going to AT&T and the other long distance carriers was going down. That could only mean that the local companies were making even more money than AT&T had as a monopoly!

Being in the region also gave me an introduction into the AT&T attitudes towards expenses. AT&T was no longer a monopolist where spending money was the key to making more money. Yet old habits died hard. The state of Texas had started a rate case against the company to review how much we were making there. Such cases were rare, and Walsh reviewed this one with alarm because the Texas commission was hostile to us. They also were not above chasing headlines by shaking loads of money from us in these type proceedings.[28] Though Texas was not my state, Walsh asked that I help out. I drew the assignment of defending the Network and Bell Labs budgets.

States frequently went after the Labs budgets, arguing that it didn't help the people of their state that the Labs had discovered the Big Bang! Fortunately, we were able to show sufficient savings from the more mundane Labs inventions put into the network in each state that Texas backed off that particular inquiry. It was on the network side that I had my eyes opened.

After several attempts, the director (fifth level) of the regional network organization agreed to meet with me. It shouldn't have been that hard; our offices were on opposite sides of the same floor in AT&T's Atlanta Headquarters Building. She seemed to have no interest in

---

28 Rate cases were used to review whether or not a utility was making too much money, either because it was exceeding its authorized rate of return, or because its expenditures were not viewed as reasonable. Nine times out of ten, there was a political motivation that you had better understand – such as a politician trying to look good for an upcoming election.

the proceeding whatsoever, and allowed herself to be interrupted several times while I was trying to explain why the case was important. Finally, using the amount of diplomacy I thought appropriate for the occasion (*i.e.*, none), I challenged her lack of cooperation, and told her if she didn't want to submit testimony defending the reasonableness of the network budget, it was fine with me.

She stared at me, and finally broke the silence, asking me what I wanted to know.

I decided to start with the basic facts like:

"I haven't found anyone who can tell me what the Network organization budget is for Texas, or even the southern region. Let's start with that. What is it?"

I expected her to pull some secret binder out, and look up the answer. No chance. Instead she stared at me like I was an idiot, saying, "My budget is whatever I need. You don't seem to understand – this is the Network we're talking about!" She paused to let the majesty of that sink in, before continuing, "Without us there is no AT&T. We put our budget together historically. During the year we spend whatever we need to run and expand the network." Regardless of whether she were right (I think she was not; the Network had to have a budget. This was 1986, for crying out loud!), the fact that she, a high-ranking Network official felt that she had unlimited amounts of money to spend was a problem. At least it became a problem when the endless streams of money pouring into the company were reduced to still generous but finite amounts.

Old habits die hard, and the historic lack of attention paid to expenses was tough to end. Perhaps no example of waste better captures the early 1980s at AT&T than the following stories.

AT&T was a rigid hierarchy. Employee status was broken down into levels, and everything from salary to the size of one's office depended on one's level. Even the carpet outside executive offices was a richer carpet than the carpet outside other offices. An acquaintance of mine who was not then an executive was assigned an office that had a door that opened onto the better carpet. The building maintenance team sprang into action. The offending door was walled up, and a new door was cut into the adjacent wall so that the door would open onto the proper standard of carpet for someone at his level. Another time a "fourth level" attorney was assigned to a "fifth level" office, which was larger than the space to which he was entitled. Building a false wall within the office that sealed off the extra space, reducing the office to the proper size, solved the "problem!" Less dramatic but equally silly, Walsh reminded me of the time that one of his staff (a fourth level attorney) was told that his office plant was a "fifth level plant." The incorrectly assigned plant was carted away and replaced with vegetation suitable for a mere fourth level.

Waste and inefficiency were everywhere. Lawyers are known to want to change things in their papers right up to the last minute, and the attorneys that staffed our FCC group were no exception. Rather than set up an orderly process where pleadings were finished the night before they were due, and then express mailed for filing in the District of Columbia, our attorneys would make changes until late morning on the day the pleading was due. Then staff employed just for this purpose would finally be given hard copy of the pleading and run to a waiting limo, drive to the airport, fly down to D.C., and make the filing. They would then return in the same manner. Given that we made filings almost every day, this was a very expensive way to get things done.[29]

---

29 Yes, this was before emailing documents was available.

None of the above practices carried huge price tags, but they set a tone that pervaded the company. The company spent money on matters that had nothing to do with serving customers. AT&T had money to burn, and seemed content to burn it.

Chapter 10

International Growth, Joint Ventures and Investment Bankers

In 1987, after only a year and a half in the region, I found it necessary for personal reasons to relocate back to New Jersey. I didn't want to go back to writing pleadings for the FCC, so I went to talk to AT&T General Counsel John Zeglis. We had a great talk, at the end of which he said he'd see what he could do. By the time my plane landed back in Atlanta he had decided: I was the new international expert on commercial matters for Network Systems, the name we used for the part of Western Electric that made the equipment used in networks. It didn't matter that I had never done commercial work, or that my international experience was limited to backpacking through Europe before law school. This was 1987, and AT&T had announced bold plans to expand rapidly overseas. Much of this growth was expected to come from the sale of networking products. At the beginning, I pretended to know what I was doing, discovering that everyone else was doing the same thing.

The fact that AT&T was in such a rush to become a global player affected negatively the strategic choices the company made. The company didn't want to spend the decades it takes to localize its products, build sales presences, or understand the unique characteristics of each market. It wanted to be big immediately, not start small and grow gradually. It decided to do a series of joint ventures with companies that could help it grow rapidly. The thinking was that AT&T had the best products in the world; if it ventured with companies that had access to the key markets overseas, then it would have the world in its pocket.

Joint ventures are established to pool the resources of two entities to fill in some gap that each of them has among the factors needed to achieve business success. In other words, rather than taking the time to gain the capability one's self, why not blend your strengths with the strengths of another so that together the two entities can win in the marketplace?

The theory sounds great, but joint ventures are quite tricky and rarely if ever work. The reason lies in the distinction between a full merger and a joint venture. Mergers are simple: before the transaction there are two companies; afterwards there is one. With joint ventures, however, before there were two; and afterwards there are three! The parents do not merge, because the area to be addressed by the venture is a subset of the parents' activity. That makes things very difficult: operations and people have to be carved out of each parent and transferred to a new company. Complex contractual arrangements have to be put into place governing what the parents will do; what the venture will do; and how the three entities will interact. A good rule of thumb is that it takes roughly as long to negotiate a joint venture as the new entity, once operational, is likely to last.

I spent six years negotiating our joint ventures, putting them together and taking them apart. I probably had as much experience as anyone at AT&T in working on these projects, and can safely say that we never made them work for us. I don't think that we were worse at venturing than others; it is the lack of financial alignment among the three entities that is difficult to manage.

The best way to explain this is to think through the process of creating a venture. Each party contributes assets and people, creating the balance sheet and employee base of the new entity. This creates immediate distrust; the other party is no doubt doing the same thing that you are doing, and overstating the value and significance of its contribution.

After all, the value of a business operation is a very subjective thing, based on future earnings potential, which in turn is generally a projection of historical earnings, taking into account any known differences between the historic and current environments.

To place a value on the business being contributed, however, one must make a number of subjective judgments about the allocation of corporate overheads. For instance, one can make the business being contributed look as if it made a huge profit simply be playing games with the hypothetical historical overheads that go into the calculation of past profitability. How it does in the future is dependent on the real overheads with which the parents have saddled the joint venture. If it falls short, one can always blame it on venture management, who took this supposedly profitable business, and ran it into the ground! A company that tries to be noble and to honestly value the business being contributed is thought naïve, and will almost certainly be taken to the cleaners by its more worldly partner.

This atmosphere breeds suspicion, and prompts each of the partners to move deliberately (a nice word for "slowly"). Finally, however, the work establishing the venture is done, and it is up and running. Each parent gets a real insider's look at the assets contributed by the other. And, each realizes that it must share the profits of the venture. If one of the parent companies feels that it was taken advantage of in the formation process, it is likely to take action to restore a fairer balance. For instance, it may let its sales force begin poaching a bit, trying to serve the most lucrative targets of the venture rather than deferring to the venture. Which customers belong to the venture and which remain the parent's responsibility is difficult to define, and is never made completely clear in the formative documents. (Ambiguity is tolerated *then* in the interests of avoiding the difficult issues during the negotiations.) Building the annual budget for the venture becomes a theatre of the absurd exercise where distrust and bad feelings makes everyone forget why they formed the venture in the first place.

While the parents are tangled up in internal issues, the competitors continue to attack the customer base, capitalizing on the confusion and the customers' inherent distrust of the new company. Customers begin to defect. The loss of revenues doesn't fit with the increased costs of the venture, and the whole thing comes unglued.

When I arrived in 1987, Network Systems was trying to take the first steps to globalize. The formula was simple. It believed that its flagship product – the 5ESS switch – was the best network switch in the world. It probably was. Of course, Europe and the rest of the world (excluding Taiwan and Korea which had embraced the American standards) had built their telecom networks using different standards and the 5ESS would have to be modified to work in their networks. AT&T entered into a global joint venture with Philips, an "also ran" when it came to telecom products but a company that had strong national sales organizations in a number of important countries (including Germany and Spain). Under the original deal, its all-important German operation (PKI) was to be folded into the venture to give it a foothold there.

The basis of the venture was to be AT&T products sold by Philips' world-wide sales organization. The idea seemed like a good one, but it didn't work. The development costs to convert the 5ESS to European standards appalled Philips, who then reneged on the deal to fold PKI into the venture. AT&T accepted as compensation about seventy million dollars, but the venture never recovered from this miscue. Other than Philips' home country of the Netherlands, and to a lesser extent a few isolated sales in Spain and the UK, the 5ESS didn't get established anywhere else in Europe.

In 1987, AT&T (with some help from Philips) tried to break into France. The French government was auctioning off a company I only remember by its initials – CGCT. It didn't have good technology; it had too many employees and it was running short on cash to pay its bills. Yet AT&T became involved in an intense bidding war with the German company Siemens for this broken down company. Why? Because it came with a promised 13% share of the French switching market! How can one promise to award a specific percentage of a supposedly open market? The question would befuddle most scholars, but didn't trouble the antitrust sleuths at the European Commission one bit! The truth was that the French and German markets for telecom equipment were kept tightly closed and controlled by their governments. The EC – the European Commission with the antitrust responsibility to prevent that from happening -- had more sense than to disrupt such home-grown hegemony. After a lot of government-to-government discussions, Siemens was declared the winner. It got to pay a king's ransom for CGCT, the struggling French company. At the same time, it began to receive orders for switching from the French PT&T, which would eventually equal thirteen percent of its demand.

France and Germany had indigenous competitors in the network equipment market, and thus were very careful to make certain AT&T did not get a foothold in those markets. Italy did not. Italtel, the Italian equivalent of Western Electric, used Siemens as its technology partner, and most of what it manufactured was Siemens'-designed products. They had designed their own switch and were proud of it, but it was not used to any degree outside of Italy. It is fair to say that Italtel wasn't a world player.

A very short time after being blocked in France, AT&T was contacted by Italtel. Italtel expressed interest in doing a deal pursuant to which AT&T would replace Siemens as its technology partner. Its chairwoman, Dr. Marisa Bellsario, was a brilliant woman and charismatic leader, and had become convinced that Italtel's future would be brightest linked to AT&T. Sadly, she died before the venture was launched. Partly out of respect for her, her team finished the deal and the venture was created in 1989.

By the time AT&T was ready to negotiate with Italtel, I was a trusted fixture at Network Systems. I had negotiated the buyout of Philips from our joint venture, and had become counsel to both Switching and Transmission Systems, the two largest product groups in Network Systems. The head of Network Systems, William Marx, and the two leaders of Italtel, Salvatore Randi and Gianni Barbieri, developed a good rapport. Pio Cammarata, the Italtel general counsel, and I also got along famously. Sadly, however, the financials of the deal just didn't make sense without the 5ESS switch, at least from the AT&T perspective. (We had a fairly limited range of transmission products of interest to Italtel; most of what the Italians wanted required development dollars and time.) At one point during the negotiations, we made a concerted effort to re-introduce the 5ESS by essentially proposing that the Italian switch be made a "module" of the 5ESS, with our product becoming the real brains of their network. An emotional Gianni Barbieri reacted by shouting, "Don't you think I would want to bring the 5ESS in if I could? But I can't. If you don't understand that, we have nothing else to talk about." Marx flew in, dressed us down in front of the Italians, and that was that.

We had a wily veteran in charge of our Switching business for a time. Bob Carlson knew both the products and how to price them. I remember coming back with great enthusiasm from finishing the deal with Italtel, and running into Bob. I asked him what he thought about the deal. He gave me a sobering look before saying, "You don't win by partnering with losers." I wanted to protest but didn't. I knew what he meant. Italtel really didn't have what we needed – a market presence outside of Italy. And we didn't have what they wanted – a robust product line that could be delivered to them for manufacture in Italy.

A few years later the Italians pulled the plug.

After Italtel came British Telecom. This was a colossal deal on the services side, which essentially merged much of our international operations with theirs. Designed to serve the needs of large business customers, each party agreed to make the venture its exclusive vehicle to serve both large retail accounts and other carriers (i.e., our wholesale accounts). Marilyn Wasser, AT&T's corporate secretary, our normal dealmaker and a friend, called me up one day, revealed that she had been working on this deal, and told me that she was so sick of dealing with British Telecom that I was going to have to do it instead. I ended up feeling much the same way. Their businessmen didn't seem honest, and their chief lawyer and negotiator (Jack Greenberg) was deliberately offensive. When I joined the negotiations, the first thing I had to do was to explain why we couldn't do something BT wanted us to do. Marilyn introduced me and before I even opened my mouth, Greenberg said in a sarcastic stage whisper loud enough for everyone around a very large conference table to hear, "Right. This ought to be interesting," as if anything I might say after his introduction was bound to be a lie.

The night we resolved all the final issues and signed the deal, I was there with one of our corporate lawyers (Michael Berg) for AT&T. There wasn't an AT&T businessman to be found. When I came to business issues where I didn't feel like going out on a limb without company, I would call John Haig, who had worked on the deal and was a junior officer at AT&T (like myself). He had two things that made me like him: first, he was willing to take my calls. Second, John had common sense, which was an invaluable commodity on our side, because it was so rare.

I had the distinct impression that the deal was an orphan at birth. Unlike the Italtel deal where the senior executives liked and seemed to trust each other, here there was no warmth in any of the relationships that I saw. The parties simply didn't trust each other. The first year, the venture was projected to earn three quarter of a billion dollars; it lost nearly a billion dollars instead. It was terminated by both parties out of concern that the subsequent years would be even worse.

That wasn't quite the end of things, however. BT asked whether we would be interested in a broader venture, which would include the international business already committed and add to it assets and business within the United Kingdom that served the same customer set. We were. AT&T's investment bankers took the lead on these discussions. We rushed off to the UK with about fifty people to do due diligence. Our bankers had organized things so that finance people only saw finance materials, lawyers saw legal documents, and so forth. One couldn't get a good idea of the Byzantine way BT was proposing to split its operations between those that were going into the venture and those that weren't by looking at things that way.

I ignored the instructions, therefore, and spent two days going through the notebooks surreptitiously, tracking the services that the venture would get, and matching each with the historical financial results for such services. There was nothing ingenious about it; it was what you would do if you hadn't been given instructions to put on blinders before trying to see what was going on. In any event, a disturbing pattern soon emerged – the services that were big money losers for BT were all going into the venture, and the services that made them a ton of money were being kept out. That description may be a little simplistic, but only a little. We were walking into a trap!

I did not trust our investment bankers. Quite frankly, the bankers should have spotted this if they had done even cursory due diligence. Investment bankers don't get their very substantial fees unless a deal goes through, which gives them a powerful incentive to make deals happen. To avoid any filtering of the facts as I saw them, I worked most of the night on a memo, sent it about four in the morning to John Zeglis, who by then had left the ranks of lawyers and had become President of AT&T, and Jim Cicconi, who had become General Counsel and was my boss. I don't know which of them gave it to the Chairman, but by the end of the next day, the AT&T team was called home, and all further negotiations with BT ceased.

You may think my opinion about investment bankers is too harsh. I don't think it is. In fact, what I've shared thus far is fairly benign. I think the use of investment bankers is the greatest fraud on modern business that I've seen. Here's why.

Companies who want to buy other companies must justify the price they pay. If they don't, any disgruntled shareholder may sue the Board on behalf of the company and its shareholders. (Such lawsuits are called derivative actions.) Given that many transactions fail to meet their original goals, this is not a risk executives want to take. Can you imagine defending a multi-billion dollar acquisition after it has become clear that you grossly overpaid for something that doesn't work very well?

What can the poor CEO do? He sees the target company, and wants it. Tell him he can't have it and he only wants it more. What he needs is an insurance policy so that if he does get sued, he can say, "Hey, I got an independent opinion from our investment bankers, and they thought the price was fair." Then the CEO and the Board are protected by the business judgment rule – they don't have to be right so long as they exercised reasonable business judgment, which the banker's fairness opinion guarantees that they did!

You now know the role of investment bankers. Their role is not to ensure that the actions of the CEO or Board are wise, but to insulate from scrutiny all actions, wise and unwise, that the CEO and Board may take. AT&T's bankers, who should have known that AT&T could not afford the purchases it was piling on one after the other during Mike Armstrong's "acquisition hysteria"[30] are reported to have pocketed about $150 million for the fairness opinions supporting TCI and Media One, the two large cable operations that AT&T purchased. These are the same assets that AT&T sold almost immediately after it had acquired them (at a loss of more than fifty billion dollars!) because it couldn't service the debt it had taken on in connection with their purchase. I may sound cynical, but that is because the facts only allow a very cynical conclusion: the bankers knew that AT&T's cash flow was insufficient to cover all the new debt it was taking on, but supported the transactions anyway to obtain their very rich fees!

Every once in a while, a CEO wants to buy something that even the most creative banker can't find a way to justify. Like Teleport Communications Group ("TCG") a local access provider AT&T acquired in 1998 for $11.3 billion dollars. That's where the word "synergy" comes in. A word of warning: if you see a company use the word "synergy" in an SEC filing, sell whatever shares you have immediately, and whatever you do, don't buy any more![31]

Synergies plug the gap between what the CEO has agreed to pay for the acquisition and what the target, optimistically, could be worth. In other words, while the intrinsic value of the entity being bought may not be worth the price (or a tenth of the price!), the combination of its operations with the operations of other stuff you already own creates new value, called synergies. And wouldn't you know it, the synergies added to the value of the thing being acquired equals or exceeds the price paid! Don't you love it when that happens?

---

30 See, Chapter 20, *infra*.

31 The above is not intended to be investment advice. Please read all relevant prospectuses. Then, run like hell!

Here's how the process really works. Word goes out to the leaders of the internal units from whom the synergies are desired to come up with such extra value. (In this case, we are talking about my unit, Business Services.) This was not an acquisition that was being pushed, bottoms-up, by the operational leaders. Requests are sent to the sales teams to come up with as many extra synergy dollars as they thought humanly possible. The answer came back with the honest view that there wasn't much there. The answer was rejected and they were told to do it again. Part of the problem was that what TCG offered was a plethora of fiber rings, which was the access method of choice for large customers. AT&T, however, was a far more substantial builder of rings itself, and already had most of its large customers on such facilities.[32]

The other problem was that agreeing to synergies meant that whatever number was agreed to would be added to the business plan, and those agreeing were responsible for meeting the original plan, plus the additional synergies. That's all very logical, right? The reality, however, at least at AT&T during the Armstrong era, was that there was such intense pressure on the traditional units to sign up for business plans with sufficient profits to fund the purchases in the first place that they were severely stressed trying to make the original plans. Adding generous amounts of synergy to make a purchase possible was not something anyone in the business unit wanted to do, especially when the business to be acquired was not profitable!

Still, it was done. The bankers had convinced the Chairman that this was a wise purchase and that made it a "done deal." There was a lot of muttering but no open dissent. Most of the managers seemed to

---

32 Rings offered two benefits: first they allowed the companies using them to avoid access charges (since they were direct-connected to AT&T and didn't go through a local switch; and second, rings provided two paths for signals, meaning that it would take two simultaneous cable cuts to put a location on the ring out of service. For many businesses, that added measure of safety was essential.

know that the company was headed for the brink. So they bought time, while most of the high level management who knew what was going on began to look for employment elsewhere.

Chapter 11

Managing the Budget Process in a Crisis Environment

People crave normalcy. Even in a business that is plummeting out of control into the abyss, there is a natural human tendency to ignore the devastation and try to manage things the way they've always been managed. So with AT&T, the fact that a new chairman was squandering billions did not derail the "normal" functioning of the budget process, at least in the beginning of each new budget year.

The process would start with the "revenue' meeting. This was an oasis of optimism. New programs would be started, new product commitments would be made, new ideas would be black-boarded for further study, and the development community would be pressed to sacrifice efficiency for speed. Man, the new products sounded like dynamite. The sales teams built plans to hit the markets with renewed enthusiasm. One would leave those meetings charged up and ready to turn the world on its head. Anything was possible!

Invariably, however, the "cost" meeting would be held soon after. It normally would be kicked off by someone from Finance, who would be brief and come right to the point. The sky was falling. Past promises of increased revenues had not panned out, leaving the finance team deeply disappointed in everyone in the room. Heads would hang. Now, the company had little choice but to cut costs quickly and drastically. And, because half the time had passed before the company's next quarterly report, the cost cuts now would have to be twice as deep in order to deliver the needed cost savings in the time remaining. Every program initiated in the revenue meeting was scrapped, the money invested to that point wasted. Then the real fun would begin.

To make budget cuts intelligently, one should prioritize spending across organizations, cutting the least important spending first. Lucky is the businessman who has anyone in his company who is willing to acknowledge that what they do with their few budget dollars isn't the most important thing going on in the entire corporation, if not the most important thing imaginable. Nonetheless, efforts are made to avoid the mindless across-the-board cuts made in previous years and to do it right this year! After spending precious time trying to find the budgets with low priority, the finance team concludes there is no better alternative than to cut all budgets across the board. It may not be fair or the best, but it can be done quickly.

Of course, there are those organizations that at the beginning of each year build some extra "fat" into their budgets in anticipation that this might happen. The discussion becomes heated as allegations that this was done are made. Cries of passionate disagreement echo through the room,

"Did not!"

"Did too."

"Did not. Besides you did it more!"

"Did not!"

"Did too." At the end of the day, no one is happy, and each organization vows silently to build even more fat into their budget submissions next year.

While most knew how to play the budget game, few were prepared for the draconian impact of Armstrong's harvest attitude towards the traditional business. *The threshold for new capital investment became in-year payback!* In other words, suppose you were in sales and could add three customers if AT&T were to construct a fiber ring that passed their locations. If the costs to do so exceeded the return you would realize *the same year*, you would need to obtain special approvals to get the project funded.

Compare the manner in which Armstrong analyzed the purchase price of acquisitions and you see the bias against internal growth. Armstrong was willing to pay more than twenty times annual revenues for a business that had never made a dime of profit (TCG); but the core business was not given capital unless it could demonstrate virtually immediate profitability.

It didn't take a genius to figure out that if one were at AT&T and therefore couldn't be bought, one nevertheless had to find a way of separating one's self from the core business so as to qualify for the looser standards applicable to new business! This of course brings us to Rick Roscitt, and the internal start-up called "AT&T Solutions."

Chapter 12

AT&T Solutions Solves Nothing

Most of AT&T's large customers developed large IT/telecom departments to manage their computer and other networks. Some, like IBM, built their own private networks on a global basis. As these operations became more and more complex, customers became interested in having someone else run their networks for them. "Outsourcing" was born. The basic outsourcing package would involve the outsourcer taking assets and people from the customer, removing those assets from the customer's balance sheet, and then providing back services under a long-term contract. The key to the whole arrangement was to provide those services more efficiently so that the customer would save money at the same time the outsourcer made money.

AT&T went into the outsourcing business out of concern that if its customers selected another outsourcer, that company might treat transport as a commodity item, selecting a "cheaper" carrier to provide it. It was termed "disintermediation" and it was a bad thing.

Rick Roscitt, the AT&T executive who studied the matter, convinced Armstrong of the need to set up a separate unit to combat this scourge, and promised that if given freedom from the demands of immediate profitability, he would grow the business rapidly to five billion dollars from nothing in three years! Armstrong readily agreed and AT&T Solutions was born. The management team of the new unit would be richly rewarded if the revenue target were met, whether or not the unit had made a dime of profit.

Revenues did take off as AT&T Solutions signed a number of large customers to outsourcing deals. It's unclear how much was truly new revenues and how much was the old telecom services bundled in; that didn't matter – Solutions was flying high. When Roscitt proposed buying IBM's global network for five billion dollars, Armstrong approved it, even though there was a nagging issue that its purchase violated the exclusivity provisions of the just-signed deal with British Telecom. (It clearly did violate those terms; but BT never made a stink over it.) There was an even bigger nagging issue whether this was the best use AT&T could make for five billion dollars, but this project (for which our bankers would reap rich fees) had the support of our bankers, whereas investing in our existing business such as wireless (which would not enrich those bankers) did not enjoy the same degree of enthusiasm.

Compensation plans drive behavior. The flaw in the compensation design here was obvious, and the Solutions team had a field day signing contracts that were not profitable unless much greater efficiencies, not supported by any plan, fell from the sky. The customer signed because he received savings in the early years. But once those savings were realized, there was nothing else to throw at the customers to keep them happy. As a result, one by one, the Solutions contracts became bones of contention with the customers. Rather than drawing them closer, the Solutions business alienated a number of very large customers. But I am getting ahead of myself. This was predictable but not otherwise apparent the first couple of years. Roscitt was making revenues go up, and Armstrong liked that.

At the same time, Business Services revenues were going down. Armstrong was not investing in this business; rather it was being used as a cash cow to fund other ventures. Michael Keith, then President of Business Services, had an annoying habit of being honest about what the unit could do, and kept telling Armstrong that it could not deliver the 2000 profits that Armstrong wanted. Armstrong replaced Keith with Roscitt.

Suffice it to say that Roscitt and I did not have a great relationship. During the negotiations with IBM to buy their global network, I asked to see the term sheets that were being negotiated largely through outside counsel. There were proposed terms that Roscitt had agreed to that presented risks to us significantly greater than we normally assumed. I recognized that I had little chance of stopping anything, but I did write a short memo to Somers, the AT&T CFO, to try and start a discussion. (At that point, I didn't know Somers well enough to realize that complaining to him about commercial terms was a pointless exercise.)

A short time later, I attended a holiday party thrown by Armstrong. Michael Keith and I were sitting at a table with our wives (Keith had not yet been replaced by Roscitt, though that would come soon.) Roscitt came to the table and asked to talk to me privately. I got up and we took a few steps away so that we would not be overheard. He told me that Somers had given him a copy of my memo. Without discussing the substance of it, he then said that many people would consider the fact that I sent it as showing I was not a team player. He told me that he had defended me this once, but that if I were to do something like this again, he wouldn't protect me a second time. It was an elegant threat.

Roscitt had campaigned hard for the top position in Business Services; ironically he succeeded just as the wheels were coming off the bus. Business Services was in crisis with revenues and average revenue per minute ("ARPM") both going in the wrong direction. ARPM was something we watched carefully because our small business customers, who paid the highest prices, were also the most vulnerable to RBOC entry into long distance. As we lost small business customers, the

ARPM would naturally fall. Armstrong asked for an in-depth review of the business, recovery plans and the like.

At the review, Roscitt gave a short introduction, and then turned the presentation over to his team. Roscitt sat next to Armstrong and proceeded to outdo the Chairman in asking tough questions, challenging his team and acting as if he were hearing the bad news for the first time.

Dave Dorman, our next chairman, knew the telephone business and wasn't as easily fooled as was Armstrong. He later told me that he forced himself to take 45 days to size up his top lieutenants, of which Roscitt was one. He fired Roscitt on day 44.

Chapter 13

I'm Shocked, Shocked to Find Bribery Going On Here!

The New York Times carried a story in 2007 about the German company Siemens paying bribes in order to secure business in Saudi Arabia. That's hardly news. During the time I worked for AT&T's equipment group (1987-1993), bribery in the sale of telecom equipment was rampant and was the common practice not only of Siemens, but of most European and Asian companies. Only the U.S. companies, or at least those that (like AT&T) really did try to comply with U.S. law, refrained from making the payments expected by customers in countries where such practices were prevalent.

In Saudi Arabia, there is a peculiar irony to the allegations against Siemens. Siemens did well there, and that meant that its agent had to have been the recipient of large payments in the past that it did little or nothing to earn. Siemens, while no innocent, must have done something truly shocking (like telling the agent "enough already!") to warrant being dragged by the Saudis through the press.

Saudi law builds bribery into the system, making it a crime for a foreign company to sell products directly into Saudi Arabia without an agent. The agent's compensation is also set by law – usually at five percent of the value of the products sold. That means that five percent of the value of all the weapons, all the telecom products, and all of everything else sold in the country by foreign companies is paid to an agent whose job it is ostensibly to help foreign companies obtain business. Consider it a tithe to the royal family, for that is what it is.

U.S. law, specifically the Foreign Corrupt Practices Act, makes it illegal for U.S. companies to make payments to officials of foreign governments for the purpose of obtaining or retaining business. U.S. corporations acting overseas dutifully ask that their agents sign contracts that have a clause specifying that the payments they receive are for services rendered, and will not end up in the pockets of foreign officials. Applied in Saudi Arabia, however, this is absurd. *The government was and is the royal family, and the agents were almost all princes in it!* No, they don't hold official titles, in deference to their American clients. But money paid to a prince is money paid to "the family." The notion that these princes earn the millions in fees they collect was officially put to rest for me when the reason why AT&T wasn't awarded a particular project in Saudi Arabia was that "it wasn't our prince's turn" to win a project. We were told to be patient; his (and our) turn would come soon. We were, and it did.

American companies are both resented and considered naïve for trying to comply with U.S. law. The resentment is due to our country's attempt to legislate how business should be done in another country. The charge of naiveté is a reflection of the facts that in some countries (particularly many in South America, Africa and the Middle East), it was next to impossible to do business without making such payments. The more worldly French had a better attitude about such things: their laws prohibited bribery, but only in France. They certainly did not want to dictate the way business was conducted outside their borders.

Ironically, our government takes the exact opposite view: it is perfectly legal, for instance, to make a big campaign contribution to influence the award of government contracts *in this country*. It is a criminal offense to make the same payment for the same purpose to a legislator in another country. U.S. law reflects that noble sentiment that charity, or more particularly, bribery, should begin at home.

In any event, the fact that we tolerate at home the same things we condemn abroad makes that condemnation seem very hollow to most observers from other countries, who find the U.S. position laughable. If we want anyone in the world to take us seriously, we owe it to the U.S. companies who are trying to compete globally to require of our own officials the same standards we think appropriate for officials in foreign countries.

Alcatel, the former ITT subsidiary that bought Lucent and the Labs in 2006 (see Ch. 14, *infra*) was frequently accused by the AT&T sales force of paying bribes to win business. While it is possible that these reports were simply excuses to explain why AT&T hadn't won, they were presented me with such passion and supporting embellishments that they appeared credible to me. It wouldn't have been surprising in any event; this was the way business got done in a large part of the world. Nor was Alcatel a company afraid to ignore the law. On another occasion, they had proposed to AT&T's submarine systems unit[33] that we rig bids so that each company could make even more money than before. Fortunately, the head of our unit let me know what they had proposed. The fact that he came to me in the first place indicated that he wanted no part of their scheme; my promise to visit him in prison if he went along with it let him know my views. He turned them down.

The laws prohibiting bribery can be tricky; U.S. law doesn't prohibit all bribes but only those that are made to "obtain or retain" business. So-called "facilitating payments," payments made in order to induce a government official to perform some ministerial act that is not itself illegal are perfectly fine, provided the American company accounts for the payments correctly.

---

33 Submarine Systems was the name given to our fleet of ships that maintained the undersea cables. It was an extremely lucrative business because of the large number of undersea cables, and the fact that there were only two companies that were capable of doing such maintenance – AT&T and Alcatel.

AT&T had built a number of projects in Egypt financed by the Agency for International Development, and had completed one particular project that was ready for final inspection and acceptance. The problem was that the inspectors refused to go visit the site unless they were provided cars to take them there, lunch, and a truly small amount of pocket money. This was a classic facilitating payment, which it would have been legal to pay so long as it was accounted for properly.

The AT&T project manager, an experienced and highly competent man who had been overseas for the company for several years, made the payments. He asked his finance support how to record the expense but the finance man didn't know.[34] The project manager assumed (incorrectly) that he had done something wrong, and therefore accounted for the payments as sales expense, which was an incorrect entry that had the unfortunate effect of making the original payments unlawful.

The matter percolated up through finance ranks, and was finally brought to me. I was sympathetic because the facts indicated that the wrongdoing had been inadvertent, and there had been no effort to bribe someone at company expense or to bribe someone to obtain business. The FCPA has self-reporting requirements, but I felt reasonably comfortable that we could explain what happened and escape any adverse U.S. government response. Unfortunately for the project manager, however, Rich McGinn had just replaced Bill Marx as head of AT&T's network equipment business and upon my explaining the case to him, he surprised me by insisting that the project manager be fired! He told me that we must take a "zero tolerance" standard when it came to failures to comply with legal requirements. The project manager was fired.

---

34 This is less strange than it seems. The requirement here is a creature of the FCPA, and is not driven by any classic accounting rules.

I remember this incident so vividly because I found it so disturbing. The project manager had not intentionally violated any law, and had even asked the right questions with respect to the proper accounting. Under such circumstances, I found McGinn's response needlessly harsh. Later, when it became apparent that McGinn had presided over the misstatement of Lucent revenues, the gap between word and deed raised a real question of his integrity, at least in my mind.

Chapter 14

"Trivestiture," and the Demise of Lucent

In 1996, AT&T divided itself into three pieces by divesting itself of two of its pieces: NCR and its Network Systems business (i.e., the former Western Electric), which it renamed "Lucent." Lucent included Bell Labs. Both Lucent and NCR were spun-off to investors rather than being sold to a third party.[35] The spin of Western Electric was done to free it from the friction caused by the fact that its chief customers – the RBOCs – were the chief rivals to AT&T's service business, and this was hurting Lucent's sales. NCR was spun at the same time because AT&T wanted nothing more to do with the computer business, and the spin of Lucent offered a public relations smoke screen that AT&T hoped would deflect too many hard questions about the company's computer history.

Trivestiture marked the end of any pretense that the company's strategy negotiating the MFJ had made any sense. That which the company had feared – the loss of Bell Labs – the company now embraced voluntarily. That which the MFJ gave it the freedom to do – to enter the computer market – the company now exited never to re-enter. The bold statements of market convergence, of the melding of computing and communications in such a way that AT&T would achieve greatness, faded from view. More than anything else, trivestiture marked

---

35 Each existing AT&T shareholder received shares in the new concerns. While potentially better for shareholders, it also meant that the parent company got no compensation for the loss of whatever value the units divested may have had for it.

the first public acknowledgement of AT&T's strategic confusion. In 1984, AT&T had told investors that the markets for communications and computing were merging into a market it had called "information services." It had also told the world that within five years, twenty-five percent of its revenues would come from overseas. Now it was getting rid of its computer business and its network equipment business – the only business that really had any significant sales overseas. What did it all mean? AT&T didn't say.

All of this was forgotten for the moment, however, due to the meteoric performance of Lucent's stock price. It's hard to be critical of a decision to spin its equipment business when Lucent's share price went up more than a thousand percent, as it did. The original purpose of making Lucent independent -- to free it from AT&T so that Lucent's biggest customers, the RBOCs, would buy more freely -- seemed to be working. Revenues took off!

Increasingly over the years prior to Lucent becoming independent, the friction between AT&T and the RBOCs had caused major problems for Lucent. The RBOCs were concerned that they would be treated as second-class citizens with respect to the terms on which they procured equipment. If they had only known how much better than its parent (AT&T) Lucent treated them!

The late Bill Bickham, a friend and the chief financial officer of the Switching Business Unit came into my office one day. I was the chief counsel for AT&T's Switching Systems Business Unit (and the only dedicated lawyer they had), so we spent a fair amount of time together. He asked if I had heard about the latest reorganization within Switching, and I told him yes. Switching was going to form sub-units and track their financials for the three sub-units formed. This was 1988-89, and it was popular to organize by customer set. Here, the sub-units would be: the internal AT&T customer; the domestic market other than

AT&T; and the international market. Bill took out a sheet of paper and showed it to me. It was a set of pro forma financial results for the three units, and it showed that more than one hundred percent of Lucent's profits were coming from the internal customer! International was losing money, and the RBOCs had so leveraged their suppliers that Lucent's sales to them had become little better than break-even. Bill's concern was that a regulatory commission would look at this and find that AT&T had broken its commitment to treat the internal customer as its most favored customer.

Despite appearances, I told Bill we were okay. The language we used with regulatory commissions was that we would treat the internal customer as well as our best customer "under like circumstances." AT&T the service provider used monster switches – the 4ESS switch – designed as a long distance or toll switch to handle huge volumes of calls. AT&T had 144 of them, and was essentially the only customer that bought them. In a world of plummeting prices for network switches, AT&T reduced the prices of the 5ESS switch, designed by Bell Labs as a local switch and probably the most technologically advanced switch in the world, to just above costs. This was what the RBOCs bought. At least while I was there, Lucent raised the prices of the 4ESS product line like clockwork twice a year. AT&T did, in fact, receive the lowest prices of any customers that bought the 4ESS. That just didn't mean very much.

Shortly before Lucent was spun, it's leader, William Marx, was replaced by Rich McGinn. I was unfamiliar with McGinn, other than the fact that he had been high up in Data Systems, and therefore had an unenviable track record (given the disastrous performance of that unit). The other "power" at Lucent was Carly Fiorina. I became her lawyer during her initial assignment there, that being international market development. I respected her as being tough, and good at marketing (herself as well as the company's products, her critics would argue).

My time on the equipment side was drawing to a close, however. My immediate boss there (Keith McClintock) was replaced with Richard J. Rawson III, who had been doing regulatory work on the services side. I had liked *and* respected McClintock. Rawson was hard to dislike, but sadly, also hard for me to respect. He was thoughtful to the point of missing windows for giving advice, and didn't seem tough enough to deal with the factory-types who ran the place and occasionally had to be "smacked upside their heads." He was a good person, and under the right circumstances could have been a good general counsel. The cards he was dealt had major problems, however, and he was unable to prevent those problems from damaging the company.

When AT&T's plans to spin Lucent were announced, I went to see Zeglis. I told him frankly that I didn't want to trade him for Rawson as my general counsel and asked to come back to AT&T. Rich Rawson, on the other hand, asked me to come be the number two lawyer in Lucent, which under different circumstances, would have been attractive.

Personalities aside, it looked like AT&T had done something right by spinning Lucent. Lucent's stock price headed for the stratosphere, propelled by burgeoning sales. A closer look would have revealed that all was not well. In order to generate sales, Lucent began acting without business discipline. Hardware sales were priced without margin, and for the first time the company began pricing its software in a manner that included future license fees in the current price.

The software that drives the digital switches such as the 5ESS is immensely complex, consisting of millions of lines of code. Software pricing traditionally followed the razor and razor blades model: there would be an upfront license fee to be sure, but the real money was derived through annual Right to Use (RTU) fees. These fees generated virtually all of Lucent's profits. For the RTU fee, the customer would get new features, as well as maintenance and enhancement of the existing software. With at least one major customer of which I was aware, Lucent began selling the software, including future updates, for one-time lump sums. How do you continue to grow revenues when you do that?

A second tactic was to pay new entrants to take Lucent product. Granted, Lucent may have used different words to describe this, but what else do you call financing arrangements that cover one hundred and thirty percent of the purchase price? Many of these companies were thinly capitalized and these deals were done without effective means for Lucent to recoup its financing if (as many in fact did) the companies went belly up.

The above actions were commercially stupid. When stupidity was not enough, Lucent went beyond stupid and committed fraud. Lucent made the decision to "stuff the channel." Lucent used distributors to sell many of its products, and Lucent pushed a great deal of product to the distributors in 2000, without identifiable customers who were prepared to buy the products. Lucent took credit for the "sales" in 2000, but the distributors then pushed the unsold product back to Lucent in 2001, as they had a right to do under their contracts.

I was told that Carly Fiorina attended the meeting at which the decision to stuff the channel was made. This would mean that Lucent had been doing this much longer, as she left Lucent to become CEO of Hewlett Packard in July of 1999. While this is possible, I have not been able to confirm it. Also, during the time I worked with Carly, she was always careful to solicit and follow legal advice. I don't know in this instance the availability of legal advice, or even if the actual decision was hers. What is known if what Lucent did, which was wrong, and that its actions should have been stopped, but were not.

What Lucent did here was very different from the lawful "tricks" Lucent used while I was there. Lucent used to have huge sales in December, amounting to a "thirteenth month," when it was necessary to make the year's financial targets. Our sales contracts normally provided that title would pass (that is, the sale would take place) "FOB" or Free on Board. This meant that the product *under contract to an identified customer,* would be loaded onto the trucks of the carrier performing the delivery function, and that the trucks had left the factory. In my day, there were years in which the trucks were loaded and pushed ten feet away from the loading docks on the last day of the year. In this way, sales that would have been booked under normal circumstances in January would take place the previous December. This influenced the timing of when revenue was booked; stuffing the channel, on the other hand, was an artificial way of making revenues appear larger than they really were. That's a no-no.[36]

In November 2000, Lucent announced that it had overstated earnings by at least $125 million. That number grew to nearly seven hundred million dollars when the dust settled. Did McGinn know? Almost certainly; the decision to book as sales the unusually high volumes of product "sold" to distributors and then sold back due to lack of customers was not supportable from an accounting perspective and

---

36 I remember being called by a frustrated sales team that had made a large equipment sale in Mexico. Interested in getting the sales acknowledged for commission purposes during the current year, they had prevailed on the factory to load the equipment onto the trucks, which were then backed away from the loading docks just before midnight on December 31. They were complaining because the finance organization (which at that point still had my complete respect) told them they couldn't book the revenues. I agreed with finance. When they made the sale, our sales team agreed that Telmex would take title and incur the obligation to pay *"upon Customer Acceptance."* Thus, there was no particular significance to getting the goods on board the truck; this was not an FOB sale! I used this example trying to teach (without much success) other sales teams that the words we used in our contracts were there for a reason and that they at least ought to ask before making changes on their own.

almost certainly would have originated outside of finance. It also was critical to Lucent's making its forecast for year, and was fraught with risk. The point is that this was not an insignificant decision that would have been made at a lower level. It is extremely unlikely that this would have been done without the active involvement and support of the leaders of the business. At the very least, McGinn would have, and clearly should have, known.

The booking of revenues when they didn't have customers they could expect to buy the extra products they were pumping into the channel was not only unwise, but was unlawful as well. To book as revenues product shifted to distributors that Lucent had no realistic prospect to sell to customers is fraudulent. For whatever reason, however, the Securities Exchange Commission chose not to sue either the company or any of the individuals involved.

Lucent's legal and finance teams, the usual watchdogs over corporate behavior, didn't raise their voices until it was much too late. Jim Lusk, the Lucent comptroller, and whose job it was to make the decision on whether to book the transferred product as revenue, missed the call, with devastating consequences. When the public disclosure of over-stated revenues was made, the revelation had a catastrophic effect on Lucent's stock price. It plummeted from its high point reached in 1999 of two hundred and fifty-eight billion dollars and kept falling, reaching less than sixteen billion in 2003. Lucent struggled a bit further, before being bought by Alcatel in 2006 for slightly less than fourteen billion dollars.

In five years under McGinn's stewardship, the venerable hundred-year old company was driven into the ground. Not only did Lucent lose more than two hundred billion dollars in shareholder value, but the cumulative effect of all of its unwise commercial decisions hit hard, and Lucent had to lay off tens of thousands of employees to cut costs.

In the midst of the lay-offs, McGinn "invested" forty million dollars in a golf course, where the only members would be McGinn himself and about thirty other high-ranking Lucent executives. The Lucent Board finally acted and dismissed McGinn, but at the same time gave him a severance payment of twelve and a half million dollars, on top of a pension of one million dollars a year. Why they bestowed this largess on him is unclear; McGinn's performance clearly didn't warrant such a rich reward. The Lucent Board is as culpable as McGinn in giving the money to him.

AT&T had many faults, but over the years always acted with the highest integrity in keeping and recording its books. The credit for this belongs squarely with the Finance Group. The company was pilloried by Wall Street analysts who could not understand why AT&T could not seem to pull the financial rabbits out of its hat that competitors like MCI seemed to make materialize. True, MCI WorldCom eventually disclosed that it had horribly misstated its financials for years in what was the largest bankruptcy filing in U.S. history, but this did nothing to lessen the pain for AT&T, who had laid off thousands of workers trying to match the financial metrics of its competition. The pressures on AT&T to misstate its revenues were at least as great as they were on Lucent. Throughout my twenty-one year tenure, however, AT&T never failed to adhere to the highest ethical standards in keeping its books, thanks to the integrity of its financial team that resisted all attempts to describe our financials in any way other than what they were.

A particularly compelling example of this was the accounting treatment given to IRU (Indefeasible Rights to Use) sales. IRUs were long term leases (typically twenty years) sold by one telecom company to another, granting the buying party capacity along a certain route so that it didn't have to build its own facilities. Particularly with the emergence of fiber cables, where multiple high-capacity fibers would be placed along a given route, such arrangements made economic sense.

MCI, Qwest, and Global Crossing all at one time allegedly claimed one hundred percent of the lease proceeds the year the lease was signed, rather than as proper accounting would require, taking one twentieth of the revenue each year of the lease.

AT&T's finance team, and in particular the comptroller Nick Cyprus, came under tremendous pressure from our sales teams to do the same. To his credit, Nick refused to budge and AT&T kept its accounting accurately. When news broke that at long last the SEC had begun investigating the other companies, AT&T CEO Dave Dorman walked into Cyprus' office, kissed him on his head, and walked out, saying as he left, "Thank you for saving our company." At its best, AT&T was that kind of company.[37]

There is little good one can say of trivestiture. NCR, cured of its pretensions to become a major player in the computer market, has gone back to being a supplier of automatic teller machines to the banking industry. Those elements of the data systems business that didn't go with NCR when it was divested were closed down by AT&T. Lucent faired much worse, being bought for scrap value by Alcatel. The Labs fared worst of all. Its basic research budget went from over three hundred million dollars to zero, and this once Camelot-like institution for high tech scientists and dreamers is now a very different and lesser place. This bitter truth, of course, doesn't prevent both "AT&T" and Alcatel from crowing about the company's legacy and the heroic record of accomplishments of the Bell Labs of yore. For shame!

---

37 At the time Quest was being investigated, someone in their network group approached Frank Ianna, the leader of AT&T's Network Organization, proposing changes to some capacity-sharing agreements between the companies. They asked us to make what they called "non-substantive house-cleaning modifications." Ianna called me and I reviewed their proposed changes, which appeared to be ones designed to convert a cost sharing agreement into a sales transaction that might have supported recognition of revenue. We declined.

Chapter 15

The International Services Business, or Why Free Trade is a Myth

Zeglis brought me back to the International Services Business in 1993. This was a highly profitable area for AT&T, but one that had ground-rules that made us very vulnerable both to our foreign "partners" and to domestic competition. AT&T was an accident waiting to happen.

The provider of telephone service in every country except the United States was a monopoly, either owned or controlled by the government. Called PTTs (Postal Telephone and Telegraph companies), they were the exclusive providers of all communications services within their respective countries. International calling was conducted under rules of cooperation that had been developed by a branch of the United Nations, called the International Telecom Union. The glue that held this together was a revenue sharing arrangement using what were called "Accounting Rates." These rates were meant to represent the price charged to the calling party, with one half of the accounting rate (this fraction called the "settlement rate") paid to the foreign carrier (in the case of a U.S. outbound call) as compensation for terminating the call.

For instance, if your aunt in New York City were to call her sister in London on an AT&T line, then AT&T would be deemed to carry the call halfway towards London, and BT would be deemed to carry the call over its facilities the rest of the way. AT&T would bill the customer, and then pay an "international settlement rate" to BT for each minute. If the call originated with the sister in the UK, the same settlement rate would be paid, only this time by BT to AT&T. Each carrier owned essentially a half circuit permitting the call to be made in either direction.

The good news was that the settlement rates were so high that they offered ample profits and incentives so that the carriers were willing to invest in the laying of international cables. As a result, the ownership of cables was broad-based, with one telecom company, often AT&T, taking the lead and a large number of PTTs also investing. The bad news is that this arrangement ceased working when one of the parties introduced competition and the others did not, which is what happened.

The prices for international calling had been very high when the accounting rates were negotiated, reflecting the high costs of constructing the initial international cables in the 1950s and 1960s. Accordingly the accounting rates had been set at high levels as well. For many years, the accounting rates remained high, because of the absence of competitive forces driving prices down. For instance, accounting rates *per minute* in 1995 were still $2.20 for Pakistan and Saudi Arabia; $2.60 for Russia; and $1.50 for Nigeria.[38]

The arrangement worked well when both countries maintained telephone monopolies with comparably high international rates, and traffic volumes were more or less balanced between calls to and from the U.S. But when the U.S. introduced competition into international

---

38   The settlement rate, or the amount a carrier would pay on the amount of traffic imbalance, was half the accounting rate. For instance, if we sent the Saudis one million minutes and they sent us one hundred thousand minutes, we would pay 900,000 x (1/2 of $2.20) or $990,000. Some might remember that AT&T dedicated a satellite for our soldiers to use during Desert Storm. After being criticized for charging regular rates, AT&T reduced the prices on calls placed by our soldiers. The Saudis, however, did not agree to any reductions, and continued to collect $1.10 from AT&T for each minute. (USA Direct, the service used, is considered a U.S. outbound call for accounting rate purposes.)

services in the 1980s, things began to change dramatically. Prices for international calling began coming down in the U.S. On the other hand, prices for service to the United States barely budged, since in almost all cases the foreign carrier was a monopoly, partly owned by the government, and permitted no competition.

The burgeoning volumes of calls at lower prices from the U.S. and the resulting imbalance of traffic made the high settlement rates a cause of great concern to U.S. carriers. So-called "turn-around services" like AT&T's USA Direct allowed customers while traveling abroad to call the U.S., but be billed as if it were an outbound call from the U.S. This, however, only added to the outflow of cash to government controlled foreign telephone operators. Moreover, those payments were going up each year. In 1987, the total U.S. out-payment by U.S. industry to foreign PT&Ts was $1.67 billion dollars, because so many more calls were being made from the United States to foreign countries than the other way around. The net payments made by U.S. carriers increased to $3.7 billion dollars in 1993; $4.29 billion in 1994; $4.94 billion in 1995; and $5.65 in 1996. In 1996, Telmex (the Mexican carrier) received the largest U.S. payments, totaling $875 million. This was without any supporting economic logic, given that Mexico was our neighbor, and didn't require expensive undersea cables or satellite circuits to complete calls.

AT&T did not seek FCC help immediately. Why? Because despite the accounting rate issue, international calling was still an incredible moneymaker for AT&T, and the company preferred to try to fix things itself. Though this isn't precise, international calling in the 1980s represented about ten percent of AT&T's minutes, twenty percent of AT&T's revenues, and thirty percent of AT&T's profits. Even in 1996, international minutes were six percent of the total but represented twenty percent of the company's profits. God must take care of fools, for the huge profits co-existed with some of the worst management imaginable.

There were several things wrong with AT&T'S international business, long ignored by senior management. First, the economics of long distance calling varied from country to country, depending on the accounting rates and the traffic balances in any given country. Yet AT&T had never managed it this way. Until the mid-1980s, AT&T used average rate schedules covering large numbers of countries, so that while *on average* it made tons of money, underneath that headline there were still over a hundred countries where AT&T was losing sometimes substantial sums. Thanks to the efforts of one mid-level manager (Tom Luciano), AT&T finally began doing cost studies in 1987 on a country-by-country basis so that it could move to country-specific pricing on a profitable basis for every country.

A second disaster waiting to happen was presented by the agreements setting forth the accounting rates between AT&T and its foreign correspondents. The agreements had no termination dates, meaning as written the accounting rates never expired, but went on in perpetuity. Here again, Luciano stepped in with a fix of the problem, negotiating with the foreign carriers to put dates into the agreements. Though the PTTs didn't realize it until it was too late, this shifted the balance of negotiating power to AT&T.

Or at least it should have. AT&T developed a plan to begin controlling the issue. Given that the agreements now had termination dates, AT&T would seek to negotiate lower rates. If the other side were unwilling, AT&T would allow the agreement to terminate, and then begin paying a cost-based rate. In other words, AT&T would cease paying the higher rates that the correspondent had been used to. Although AT&T ultimately executed this plan very successfully, it wasn't without severe bumps in the road.

Mexico was the biggest bump. In addition to the general problems with high accounting rates, Mexico had in addition a unique problem:

the rate wasn't symmetrical. AT&T paid Telmex a dollar a minute for each minute we delivered to them, but collected only a dime for each minute Telmex sent to AT&T. In 1989, AT&T terminated the agreement, as it had the right to do, just before the Mexican government had planned to sell Telmex to Carlos Slim. John Berndt, at the time the senior AT&T executive for International, met with representatives of the Mexican government. Berndt held all the cards – the value of Telmex was heavily dependent on the payments by AT&T, and we had a right to stop paying the inflated rates that Telmex was used to. Despite that, Berndt emerged from the meeting having made dramatic and foolish concessions. He agreed to take only a small reduction in the settlement rate (from one dollar to ninety cents per minute), maintaining the imbalance and resulting in payments by U.S. carriers the following year (1990) of over a half billion dollars. While Berndt agreed to this "only" for three years, his mishandling of the situation also made it that much more difficult to deal with Slim in the years that followed. Over the next decade, in fact, U.S. carriers paid Telmex more than seven billion dollars, which Slim used to buy mobile assets in Central and South America, and which resulted in him becoming one of the ten wealthiest men in the world! [39]

As AT&T began to fix the accounting rate issues it had around the world, another problem arose. The economics of the international voice business depended upon both outbound traffic (for which AT&T collected the customer revenues and paid out the settlement rate to the correspondent carrier) and the inbound traffic (for which AT&T received the settlement rate). With high accounting rates, the key to high profitability lay in getting the inbound traffic. But what if foreign companies could land private lines into the U.S.? All you needed was

---

39. In 2012, Slim passed Bill Gates and went to the top of the "ten wealthiest" individuals list.

a private line connected to a switch or even a PBX[40] and the foreign carrier could then bring all of its U.S.-bound traffic over the private line. No settlements need be paid! Settlements applied only to traffic carried over the public switched network, and could be avoided if carried by private lines. If this were to be approved, the net out-payments paid by U.S. carriers would have gone through the roof!

Why couldn't AT&T do the same thing? The reason was because there wasn't a country in the world that would give AT&T an operating license to provide services in their country. Without exception, every country except the United States prohibited foreign companies from providing telecom service. The United States, however, believed in what our most naïve thinkers called "free trade." We had already permitted foreign companies to provide domestic service so the international private line authority was simply an extension of existing authority, or so they said.

After spending six years on the equipment side of AT&T, trying to sell our products overseas, and then having moved to international services, where I also was involved in our trade disputes with our international competitors, I believe I can speak with some experience on "free trade." It doesn't exist in the telecom industry, except in the minds of some U.S. economists who like the theory but have never tried to find it in fact. Based on my experience, countries break into four main categories with respect to their trade with others.

First, there are countries with indigenous competitors who keep their markets firmly closed and controlled. Germany and France are perfect examples (Remember CGCT, the worthless French company

---

40 A PBX is a "private branch exchange," or the equivalent of a small switch. PBXs are generally used by large corporations in connection with private networks. They can function as a small switch.

successfully auctioned off because it came with a promised slice of the French market for telecom switches.)

The second category of countries are those who will let you sell, but only if you transfer the technology into their country and make the products there. The plan, of course, is not only to employ their own people but also to "absorb" the technology in order to develop home-grown competitors. Examples are Korea and China. AT&T did joint ventures in Korea and Taiwan to manufacture the 5 ESS Switch. The contracts had wonderful language protecting our technical information and restricting those with access to it to joint venture employees. Despite that, the Lucky Goldstar group in Korea (our venture partner) was able to announce a few years later that it had designed and developed a switch outside the venture (called the TDX) that was extraordinarily similar to the 5ESS. (The venture continued nonetheless, with AT&T pricing the components the venture needed for the manufacturing process at levels more generous than it otherwise might have done.)

The third category of countries are those countries that have no interest in becoming a competitor but whose officials want payments in exchange for sales. The Middle East (excluding Israel), and many of the countries in the southern hemisphere fall in this latter category. AT&T eventually withdrew from marketing efforts in virtually all of these countries, because they wouldn't buy from us without payments that we could not make consistent with U.S. law.

Finally, there is the United States, which normally keeps its markets fully open to all who want to sell, and *judges the effectiveness of its (lack of) policies solely on the basis of their impact on consumers.* The U.S. approach does result in an attractive consumer market, with low prices due to the intense competition here. But it also results in the elimination of U.S. "producers" over time. They are competing in their home market against competitors from markets that are closed. With the third world markets influenced by bribes, the foreign competitors can implement aggressive price strategies in the U.S., choosing to take their profits elsewhere. It is a recipe for failure for American companies, and U.S. companies have been driven out of one market after another.

The reason why this matters is jobs. Without healthy producers, we lose the better-paying jobs. Thus, over time, even the consumers begin to suffer, as their spending power is diminished. Those who can't connect the dots, those who believe in promoting consumer interests at the expense of producer interests, I call practitioners of "Teenage Economics." That is, they assume the continuation of money for consumers to spend without worrying where the money comes from.

But I digress. Here's what happened to the attempt by foreign carriers to obtain approval to land private lines in the U.S. AT&T was able temporarily to convince the FCC to deny all such applications from countries where U.S. carriers did not have "equivalent opportunities" to enter into the home market of the applicant. Since there were no markets where we could "land' our private lines, we succeeded in blocking the foreign carriers – for a time.

Our success here ultimately fell victim to AT&T's desire to get back into the U.S. cellular business. In 1994, ten years after we gave away to the RBOCs our entire portfolio of wireless licenses without a penny of compensation, AT&T decided that it had made a mistake, and that the market was attractive after all. AT&T bought McCaw, the largest non-RBOC wireless provider for $12.8 billion dollars. Getting that deal done became the number one objective of the company. British Telecom, however, had invested in that company before we had, and had the ability to block the deal. They were willing to cooperate and let the deal proceed – for a price.

Zeglis called me to tell me that high-level discussions had taken place between the two companies. BT had agreed to not block the McCaw deal from proceeding, provided that we not only cease opposing but in fact support their latest application for U.S. landing rights. Zeglis then gave me the assignment of coming up with an argument that would let BT in, while keeping every other carrier out.

The UK, while not as open as the U.S., had at least made noises about taking some of the steps necessary to open their market to competition. They had not yet done so, however. I did make up an argument that the FCC bought – for awhile – that upon application of a foreign carrier to enter the U.S., the FCC should make an immediate determination of U.S. carriers' equivalent opportunity to compete in the other country, taking into account regulatory changes in that country expected over the next 3-6 months.

We were able to argue that no country other than perhaps the United Kingdom was within "months" of implementing the changes that would be necessary for U.S. companies to compete. Thus, BT could just squeak by (because it was UK-based), but no other company could. This relief from frontal assaults, however, didn't completely ameliorate the problem, because of another practice called "refile." Refile means the indirect routing of international voice traffic through a third country. For instance, suppose the telephone company in Nigeria doesn't want to pay the high accounting rates to terminate its telephone traffic into the U.S. It could seek surreptitiously to route or refile the traffic through another country that has much lower accounting rates with the U.S., passing off its traffic as traffic from the third country. Even better, once companies from the U.K. were able to take traffic into the U.S. over private lines, these companies could act as perfect conduits to take traffic that should have paid high accounting rates to the U.S. carriers, but now would pay nothing. While there was a few old cases handled by the ITU that suggested that refile was unlawful, there was no clear answer, and the practice was rampant. At the end of the day, there was no alternative to getting the accounting rates down to cost-based rates.

As AT&T stood with its proverbial fingers in the dike, the U.S. government decided to include telecom services in the negotiation of the General Agreement on Trade in Services (GATS), an international treaty. The treaty would have enabled foreign carriers to obtain licenses to operate in this country, meaning that they could terminate their traffic in their own switches, eliminating entirely the obligation to pay settlements on their traffic. On the other hand, U.S. carriers would only be able to terminate their traffic in a small handful of developed countries. Even more amazing, the Commerce Department had taken this position in negotiations without any discussion with U.S. industry, or any real review or analysis of the impact. The position taken was consistent with principles of "free trade," but left standing would have gutted all efforts to get the payments by U.S. carriers down.

Contacted at the eleventh hour for input, AT&T convinced the U.S. delegation to at least condition access to the U.S. market on the other countries having "cost oriented" accounting rates. Then, part two of the effort to salvage a tenable position was for the FCC to interpret cost oriented to mean something substantive. At the behest of a unified base of U.S. carriers, the FCC issued its 1997 benchmarking order, stating that cost oriented did in fact mean settlement rates consistent with those in its order, which ranged from twenty-three cents per minute for underdeveloped countries to fifteen cents per minute for developed countries. This, and an active resale market using private lines, has led to the elimination of most high accounting rates. But if you look beneath the accounting rate issue at the fundamental ground rules which the U.S. accepted as part of GATS, you will find the same imbalance as exists in most markets: the U.S. is wide open to entry, and most other countries are not.[41]

History has demonstrated that acceptance of structural rules disfavoring the U.S. is rarely without pain for those companies affected. Stay tuned...

---

41 China is a great example. China didn't sign right away, but made the requisite offer to open its market afterwards, which then entitled Chinese companies to enter the U.S. market if they so choose. The Chinese market is not open in the sense that we would understand, and entry would still require partnering with a Chinese company, with terms necessarily approved by the Chinese government. The only reason why this has not presented a bigger problem is because the Chinese military has started a reseller of its own that offers low rates for terminating traffic in China that keeps the traditional telephone company "honest!" You can't make this stuff up...

Chapter 16

Wherein the Murder Weapon is Revealed

If I were to tell you that I now had to try to explain regulatory accounting to you, I suspect I would lose a number of you to other pursuits. If on the other hand, I told you that I was going to describe to you how Uncle Sam killed Ma Bell, as well as show you the actual cudgel used by the government to take more than a quarter *trillion* dollars from AT&T and give it to its competitors, hopefully most of you will stick with me. I'm going to do the latter (though the two are really the same).

"Access charges" were first implemented the day of divestiture – January 1, 1984. There were two basic kinds: switched access, which allowed the customer to dial into the public switched network to reach any other customer anywhere in the world, and special access, which generally is a high capacity pipe used by corporate customers to connect private networks to their various locations. The original rate levels were supported by AT&T, as mentioned earlier[42] for a variety of inadequate reasons: AT&T thought that high access payments by its competitors would put them out of business; that the beneficiaries of the payments were its "children" and AT&T could afford to be maternally generous because the RBOCs were legally prohibited from competing with AT&T, and therefore the money wouldn't be used against AT&T.

Each of these reasons proved wrong. The government couldn't afford for divestiture to fail. Divestiture was intended to create, and its success

---

42 See Chapter 6, *supra*.

was dependent upon, the development of competition in the long distance market. The FCC therefore took very seriously the predictions by MCI, Sprint and the other competitors that they would have to go out of business if they were required to pay anything close to what the FCC was setting as the initial level of access charges.

On one hand the FCC had the local companies saying that they would have to raise local rates without a high level of access revenues, and on the other the new competitive carriers were saying that they couldn't survive if they had to pay such high access fees. The FCC did the only thing that would satisfy both political needs (of not having divestiture appear responsible to raise local rates, while getting long distance competition started): it made the access rates very high, but discounted the charges by fifty—five percent paid by everyone but AT&T. The RBOCs also proved to be far more aggressive than AT&T had assumed. They may have been children when first conceived but they were very rich and spoiled children who were used to getting their way, and were more than happy to take on their parent.

How rich were they? Consider that the total industry bill for *interstate* access charges was over four hundred billion dollars between 1984 and 2004! Add an estimated additional hundred to one hundred and fifty billion dollars for intrastate charges and the *RBOCs easily collected more than a half trillion dollars*! Inter-exchange carriers such as AT&T paid most of this. How much did it cost them to provide it? Virtually nothing, as later cost studies showed. It was pure profit.

The FCC made a half-hearted effort to shift the collection of these charges away from the long distance industry to the actual customers, introducing an end user charge for the first time. These amounts, paid by customers to the local telephone companies directly, were supposed to be offset by reductions in what the long distance industry paid. At least, that was the theory. It didn't happen.

Virtually all of the revenues collected through the end user charge from customers were additive to the RBOCs' existing access revenue streams; there was no offsetting reduction in the charges paid by the long distance carriers! In 1984, the industry interstate access revenues were $15.1 billion dollars of which $700 million was from end user charges and $14.4 billion dollars from IXCs ("Interexchange Carriers," another name for long distance carriers). Five years later (1989), the total for interstate access revenues had reached $19.5 billion dollars; including end user charges of $4.3 billion dollars and IXC payments of $15.2 billion. In 1994, ten years after the nimplementation of the access charge systemm, the revenue total was $21.4 billion dollars of which $6.8 billion was paid directly by consumers and $14.6 billion was paid by IXCs. The FCC had said that it was going to change the way access was collected; in fact, the amounts collected from the IXCs remained remarkably constant, with the end user charge representing a new revenue stream for local exchange carriers!!

Despite the fact that AT&T quickly switched sides on this issue, and began lobbying for reduced cost-based charges, the RBOCs were successful in keeping these revenue streams high. In 2004, twenty years after the advent of such charges, and the year AT&T concluded it could no longer compete and put itself up for sale, the RBOCs were still collecting slightly more than sixteen billion dollars from interstate access charges. Adding intrastate access charges would have pushed that number to between twenty and twenty-five billion dollars. *In the twenty-one years between divestiture and SBC's purchase of AT&T, the RBOCs collected more than a half trillion dollars in access charges, of which more than a quarter trillion dollars was paid by AT&T.*

There is no inherent logic to access charges. These charges are not based on costs; if they were the total payments likely would have been single digit billions of dollars over the same period. Nor can one rationalize the charges as being value-based. From a value perspective, it makes no more sense for the carriers performing the origination/termination functions (the "end carriers") to charge the carrier who stitches the overall call together (the "middle carrier") than it would for the middle carrier to charge the ends. AT&T invested substantial effort establishing relationships with almost every carrier in the world, so that customers could pick up their phones and call anyone in the world. There is a decent argument, though AT&T never made it, that AT&T should have filed a tariff covering "call coordination and completion."

At least I thought there was. I proposed internally that AT&T file a tariff, using every tariff trick in the book, which would essentially charge the local companies for AT&T's performance of call coordination and completion services. The amount I proposed to collect would have been roughly the same amounts they charged us for access. I would have filed after five p.m., effective at midnight, with a service initiation charge due immediately, with an obligation to pay first in order to dispute the tariff. (There is precedent for each of those terms in tariffs.) I would have made the initiation fee something to be remembered, like a billion dollars per company! I suffer no illusions and realized that we would lose, but it would have given us a field day to point out that the access regime blessed by the Commission was no less idiotic. I pressed hard to do this, and to file a complaint against the RBOC's special access rates, which were well above where they should have been. After listening to the arguments between our lobbyists and me, General Counsel Jim Cicconi agreed to support the special access complaint, but not the tariff filing.

The FCC accepted as the local companies' "revenue requirement," or the amounts the local companies needed to make, the amounts that AT&T as a monopoly had given its local companies to keep local rates at five dollars a month. Sure, you could change things and collect the money in different ways, but anything that gave the local companies less than what they had received historically was unacceptable, because it *might* lead to increases in local rates. Even much later (in 2004), when the FCC tried to broker an industry consensus around access, it used as the starting point that the local companies' revenues should not be adversely affected.[43]

The situation was even worse with the so-called "High Cost Competitive Local Exchange Companies," or "CLECs." The Communications business had far more than its fair share of quick-buck artists, or companies having no mission other than to get in, get as much money as possible and get out. The high cost CLECs were companies who entered the local business not to make money from willing retail customers, but to make money off access sold to the long distance carriers as unwilling customers. They would price their access much higher even than the RBOCs, and encourage their customers to pick AT&T or another long distance company as their long distance carrier. Then, AT&T would charge the customer its usual retail price of, say eight to ten cents a minute, and the CLEC would charge AT&T fifteen or twenty cents for "access!"[44] Worse still, the high cost CLECs would pay their end-user customers to generate traffic, and then split the proceeds with them. Or they would put in "chat lines" or other means to stimulate usage.

AT&T eventually started blocking such traffic saying it didn't want it. The high cost CLECs filed complaints at the FCC, claiming that AT&T had no choice, and had to accept the traffic. The FCC ruled against AT&T, requiring the company to take the traffic, though it

---

43 Joel Lubin was AT&T's resident expert and our negotiator on access matters with the RBOCs. I disagreed vehemently with that concession, telling Joel that if we accepted that, the ball game was over and we had lost. Joel, however, had Jim Cicconi's backing, and disagreed. We made the concession, and we lost.

44 It was a difficult situation for AT&T to avoid. For instance, if a chat-line set up by a high-cost CLEC meant that everyone who called that number would trigger a terminating access charge of twenty cents, AT&T had to pay the costs for those of its customers who made the calls. The customer making the call wouldn't know anything about the access charge his call was triggering.

began taking prospective steps to reign in the worst of the CLEC rates. Once again, however, the FCC seemed to go out of its way to protect the ability of scam-artist companies to take money from AT&T.

The public never knew this was going on because carrier-to-carrier payments were invisible to anyone but the carriers involved. The situation was bad enough when the RBOCs couldn't compete in long distance themselves. But if and when the RBOCs attained the right to offer long distance services themselves, the game would be lost for AT&T if the access situation were left unresolved. Pricing in the long distance industry had become intensely competitive; with business prices plummeting to less than a penny a minute. AT&T could not compete while paying several cents per minute in access to its competitors. Either AT&T had to find some regulatory solution to bring access rates down to costs, or it had to find a way to avoid using the LEC facilities for access. If it did neither, and the RBOCs entered long distance, the company would die.

Our special access complaint should have helped some but it ran into the partisanship of Chairman Michael Powell, who killed it by refusing to act on the complaint. The FCC had previously deregulated the special access connections used primarily by large business customers. Think of special access as large, dedicated pipes, with plenty of capacity. The basis of the deregulation was the FCC finding, as phony as a three dollar bill, that the market for special access was competitive. The competition that the FCC had presumed would develop never did, and over the next several years the RBOCs took advantage of the lack of regulation *and* the lack of real competition to raise rates. Soon, the RBOCs were exceeding by large amounts the rates of return for special access that the FCC had said were reasonable when they regulated the service.

AT&T's filing challenged the RBOC rates, based on the RBOCs' own data. AT&T had a strong case, but like all such challenges to existing rates, this could only yield prospective relief. In other words, even if the rates were found unlawful, that ruling could only be applied going forward from the date of the ruling. So what did the FCC do? Absolutely nothing! It sat on the case, not ruling for or against AT&T for over a year. Each *month* that passed without action meant almost a *hundred million dollars in excess charges* that would not be refunded, giving proof to the words that justice delayed was justice denied. The FCC didn't rule on this case until both AT&T and MCI, the two largest victims and most potent critics of the overcharging, had been bought by local exchange carriers and switched positions on the filing! The FCC then ruled against the filing.

In contrast, the FCC wasted no time, not even waiting for a filing in circumstances where it was the RBOCs getting hurt. The interconnection rates for the exchange of local traffic had created an opportunity for new entrants. Some of those entering the local markets had figured out that dial-up access for computers was recognized by the network as virtually non-stop local calling. The charges for completing a local call ("reciprocal compensation") were modest compared to the charges for completing a long distance call ("access charges"), but put enough minutes together and it became a thorn worth hundreds of millions of dollars a year in the RBOCs' sides. Had the RBOCs won these customers they would have been the beneficiary rather than the victim of reciprocal compensation, but they were not as nimble as many of the companies that had sought to enter the market to provide local service.

Unlike the special access situation, this was not a case where anyone was claimed to have acted improperly. The RBOCs could have and should have petitioned for a change in the FCC rules if they didn't like what was going on. The problem from their perspective was that it would take time – certain formalities like giving everyone the chance to be heard need to be observed. So, at the very same time the

Commission was sitting on AT&T's special access petition, it issued an order changing on its own the rules regarding reciprocal compensation, and began phasing out the payments in these circumstances.

The lack of symmetry was very apparent, and confirmed what the chairman of the FCC had been saying in off the record conversations – he was a believer in inter-modal competition; i.e., competition between different industries such as cable versus telephone. He did not believe in competition between long distance and local telephone companies, which he regarded as artificial. And, as between those two industries, his differing treatment made it clear which of them he thought should survive – the long distance services could easily be offered by the local companies once the legalities of them doing so were resolved. There is really no other explanation (other than intercession of the government to pick winners and losers) for the stark contrast between the speed with which the FCC handled the reciprocal compensation issue at the same time it was sitting on the special access debacle. It was not a good time to work for a long distance company.

A description of the inanity of access charges would not be complete without mentioning the bizarre question of whether Internet telephony should pay access charges as well. These services have never (at least to this point) taken a large share of the telephone market, but they presented a real problem to the FCC because *they used the local exchange facilities in the same manner as long distance telephone companies.* Choosing political expediency over logic, the FCC aligned itself with those who warned that government should keep its hands off the Internet, and ruled that access charges would not apply, at least for the time being, to Internet-based telephony. The FCC basically punted, saying it would revisit the issue at some point in the future, but would hold off applying access charges to internet traffic for now.

AT&T's reaction was to initiate "Project Alamo." Alamo was the code name for a secret program run by our Network group that transported tons of voice traffic over an Internet backbone, delivered it into the local calling areas where the calls were to be terminated, and then delivered the traffic to the local switch for completion as local traffic. It wasn't sufficient on its own to turn the tide of battle, as AT&T did this only for a small percentage of its traffic, but it nonetheless saved hundreds of millions of dollars in access expense.

Towards the end of 2004, SBC had detected the operation and was starting to make demands for information. We moved as slowly as possible in responding, and the matter was never brought before the FCC due to the fact that SBC bought us. Had this been litigated, I have little doubt the FCC would have found our scheme unlawful, simply because if they sanctioned it, it was too easy to do. But it illustrated the crazy distinctions that the FCC was trying to make in the access system.

Despite using the terminating facilities in virtually identical ways, traffic delivered by an IP service, or a local call, did not pay access; whereas a call that traveled on a traditional long-distance network from one local calling area to another, did. Charges were imposed not because of what the local company did with the traffic once it had it, *but because of how the call was handled before it was given to the local company for completion.* By constructing a crazy-quilt of rules establishing who was to pay what to whom, the FCC was able to determine winners and losers without the public even knowing that this was being done. AT&T was required to pay billions and billions to the local companies for originating and terminating access. These same companies would then use the money to compete for customers with AT&T. AT&T's efforts to challenge the charges legally were stymied by an unsympathetic FCC, led by Michael Powell. AT&T ultimately withdrew altogether from offering long distance service to consumers in July 2004, because it could not compete for such customers given the access charge situation. With the same conditions applying at the low end of the business market, and the upper end dependent on special access, AT&T's traditional long distance business had been mortally wounded by the government's actions, unseen by all but knowledgeable observers.

Not bad for a murder weapon, eh?[45]

---

45 I used to get a kick out of hearing the Internet carriers trumpet the cost savings of internet technology, which supposedly enabled them to offer such great rates for long distance calls. It wasn't their technology that offered a cost advantage; it was the artificial regulatory distinction that required AT&T to pay access charges while exempting the Internet telephone services from any such payments that created their advantage. Otherwise, the AT&T network was more efficient.

Chapter 17

The Roaring Nineties:
Life at AT&T Through the Prism of Litigation

I was put in charge of the legal group supporting Business Services in 1993, and promoted to a full Officer a year later. Business Services was responsible for all AT&T offers to business customers. I also picked up the legal work for AT&T Solutions, our "outsourcing" arm, the AT&T Network organization, and our international operations (including both legal and international public affairs) over the next few years.

With that broad an area of responsibility, it was unsurprising that I would have gotten a fair share of litigation. As a successful company in an industry filled with companies that were far less successful, AT&T constantly was targeted by those who thought litigation was a preferable tactic to winning in the marketplace. Shaking down successful companies through nuisance lawsuits is a time-honored tradition.

For a corporate lawyer, I had radical ideas with respect to litigation that helped define my tenure. Briefly, I believe corporations settle too many cases where they should not, and fail to bring actions as plaintiff when they should. I also had formed negative views (influenced by my tutelage under David Shapiro) about the talents of big law firms, especially those on Wall Street, to try cases. Most of these firms were very good at threats, and at wearing down opponents in pre-trial skirmishing and what is called "discovery" – the process where parties are supposed to share information and documents before trial. But they didn't like to actually try cases, because they're just not very good at it.

AT&T faced literally billions of dollars of exposure from the various lawsuits brought against the company. The litigation ended up being a sideshow, because we never lost a significant case, at least not on my watch. But it easily could have gone the other way.

The 900 Service Class Actions

900 Service, in its heyday, attracted a scurrilous lot of crooks and charlatans. If you wanted someone to talk dirty to you, or to hear what your future would be provided to you with great certainty by someone who didn't have a clue, 900 service providers were happy to accommodate you. It was also a place where one could gamble if one were so inclined, by calling into numbers offering games of chance.

900 service was essentially a billing arrangement – AT&T would provide an inbound calling service like 800 service, only 900 service would not be free; the person placing the call would pay for the call, as well as whatever fee the service provider chose to impose. The genius of the service was that it enabled the person putting up the application (the service provider) to do so without worrying about how to bill and collect potentially small amounts of money from millions of different customers. AT&T had such a capability and already mailed out bills to tens of millions of customers each month. To add a line to the bill in order to collect a charge for use of 900 service cost very little extra. This made it economical for service providers to offer their services, because the daunting job of billing potentially millions of people small amounts was taken care of by AT&T. AT&T then would remit the funds collected on behalf of the service providers to them, holding back a small amount for uncollectibles.

Not all of AT&T's 900 customers were disreputable; the largest user of 900 service was the American Automobile Association. And if you are old enough to remember Saturday Night Live's "Larry the Lobster" skit where people called in to vote on whether or not Larry should be boiled, you might also remember this was supported by 900 service.

Games of chance were very popular, affording callers the opportunity to win large pots simply by calling a 900 number. Like state lotteries, however, the odds against winning were great; unlike the state-sponsored lotteries, the money collected didn't go to some worthy cause – it went into the pockets of the service providers. AT&T and MCI were both sued in Georgia by attorneys purporting to represent a class of people who had called into games of chance and lost. The cases were brought as class actions – a modern procedural invention which allows cases to be brought on behalf of large numbers of plaintiffs where the issues in common are much more significant than the issues requiring individual proof. Most judges are hostile to class actions because they generally result in large payments to the attorneys handling the cases and very little in the way of compensation to the members of the class.

AT&T's usual defense that it was not responsible for the content carried on its network, absolutely impermeable when AT&T was simply acting like a common carrier, was not effective here. AT&T was under no obligation to offer the billing service and thus could be sued for the programs it permitted to run.

Neither AT&T nor MCI had participated in the service nor had an interest in the profits made by the service provider. But AT&T had started trying to police the service providers using our service in order to try to keep out those service providers that tried to offer explicit sexual content or were not providing the service that they claimed. This was not all out of the goodness of our hearts; AT&T had been threatened with criminal prosecution by a large number of states attorney generals for offering what the states claimed was pornography, and we needed to either start policing the providers or kill the service. It was this act of supervision that plaintiffs claimed put us in a conspiracy with the service providers. It was a stretch but they wanted AT&T in the case, because we had lots of money, and the service providers typically did not.

When I assumed the Business Services job, the question of settlement was presented to me. There were three causes of concern: (1) there was enormous exposure – in the hundreds of millions of dollars, and perhaps higher; (2) the case would be tried to a jury; and (3) the trial judge was incredibly hostile and had already ruled against us on virtually everything that came before him. MCI settled for forty million dollars, and was applauded in the trade press for being prudent. Our 900 services business was considerably larger than MCI's, and a settlement based on the same principles would likely have cost us a hundred million dollars or more.

Guilt and innocence matter to me, and I did not think we were guilty of any conspiracy. I therefore met with the new head of Business Services, Gail McGovern, presented the issues as fairly as I could, and recommended that we *not* settle. Gail won my admiration in this case as in so many others, by being willing to take the risk if that is what I thought best.

Our outside counsel handling the case, a large and well-respected Atlanta law firm, first tried to convince me that I was making a terrible mistake. When they did not succeed, they approached Pat Walsh and asked him to intercede with me. Pat alerted me to the "inquiry," and I followed up with them, making it very clear that I expected them to litigate the case to the hilt.

We fought the case and took it twice to the court of appeals, which ultimately dismissed the class aspects of the case, meaning that the named plaintiffs could represent their own interests but would not be permitted to represent hundreds of thousands of other members of the class. That meant that AT&T's exposure to any plaintiff might be ten or twenty dollars, not millions. The case had been defanged, and no longer presented any risks worth worrying about.

The victory was sweet, not only because I detested the attempt to use the courts as part of a get-rich-quick scheme by my fellow attorneys, but also because in this one area, we'd beaten MCI, who had folded their tents and paid the same parties forty million dollars.

The Reseller Cases

By far AT&T's greatest exposure during my tenure was the "reseller" cases – some 48 cases filed against AT&T by small companies that entered the telephone business to take advantage of the FCC policies of the time favoring resale competition.

Once upon a time the non-discrimination provisions of the Communications Act of 1934 were interpreted literally so that everyone from the largest corporate customers to the smallest residential users paid the same rate.[46] This changed gradually with the advent of competition. MCI and others competing with us didn't have to file tariffs at all, and were able to target specific large customers, winning them with offerings tailored to them. AT&T was belatedly granted the right to compete by using custom offers, either for simple business offers (what were called contract tariffs), or very complex corporate networks (what AT&T called VTNS or Tariff 12). So long as our custom offers were open to everyone for a reasonable amount of time, the FCC ruled it would not violate the Communications Act to offer custom arrangements, including steep discounts, to individual customers.

---

46 The same regulatory framework governed telecommunications and transport. Remember when everyone on a plane paid the same price for a ticket?

The FCC had it in its head that resellers were pro-competitive because what they were supposed to do was order large tariff 12 offerings and then aggregate many smaller customers' usage levels to satisfy the volume requirements contained in the tariff. That was the theory. The facts were very different. The typical fact situation underlying the lawsuits was as follows: the reseller would order a tariff, then not pay AT&T for the service it obtained. When AT&T sought to collect, the reseller would counter-claim, alleging that AT&T was trying to put it out of business by giving it lousy service, discriminating against it and so forth.

Other resellers became adept at reading AT&T's tariffs and ordering those that were not tightly written. For instance, many of the tariffs for large customers offered signing bonuses, paid immediately, in exchange for large, multi-year purchase commitments. That, in isolation, was fine. But add a provision to the tariff allowing the customer to terminate the contract if he replaces it with an even bigger commitment (which we did) and AT&T inadvertently constructed a house of cards where the reseller would order a tariff, collect the bonus, then roll into a larger plan, collect another bonus, and so on, signing up for larger and larger plans, each time doing so without any intent to meet the commitment. The resellers knew that if push came to shove, a sympathetic FCC would likely rule in their favor on any disputes.[47]

---

47 My favorite example of FCC irrationality was a case where our tariff provided that if usage was above one stated volume, the customer was given a 10% discount. If the customer had a higher volume, the customer received a 15% discount. The reseller argued (and the FCC agreed) that AT&T should be fined for refusing to give the reseller the 25% discount it demanded. The FCC ruled that the reseller was entitled to both discounts mentioned which, added together, equaled 25%! One need only read the decision here to realize that we were not getting fair treatment from the FCC. See Notice of Apparent Liability and Forfeiture and Order to Show Cause, FCC 94-359 (released Jan. 4, 1995).

As hospitable a forum as it was to resolve disputes for the resellers, however, the FCC was not a forum where they could win major damage awards. For that the resellers needed to transition their attacks to the courts. This they did, filing antitrust case after antitrust case against AT&T. The antitrust laws triple the damages set by a jury, and require the defendant to pay the attorney's fees to a prevailing plaintiff as well. The risk to AT&T was that a single loss could start a domino effect where we would end up paying billions of dollars in damages to a large number of "me too" cases. It was therefore not a happy moment when we lost a case in Oregon federal court, on the grounds that we had given the plaintiff shoddy service on purpose, causing it delays and costing it customers.

Our factual defense was that this was a period where we gave everyone lousy service, so we treated the plaintiff no better or worse than anyone else. We therefore hadn't discriminated against it, which was a necessary part of plaintiff's proof. Though true, the jury didn't buy it, especially in light of some nasty things the FCC had to say about our treatment of resellers in general.

Fortunately, we also had a legal defense. We provided service pursuant to a tariff, and the tariff set forth the exclusive remedies in case we gave lousy service, which was a pro-rata refund of the rates that plaintiff hadn't paid anyway. Called the "filed tariff doctrine," it is the best defense a regulated utility has against claims of virtually any nature.

The district court didn't buy it, nor did the Ninth Circuit Court of Appeals, which affirmed the judgment against us. At this point, we had exhausted the appeals we had the right to seek. Appeals to the U.S. Supreme Court are discretionary with that Court (except in narrow situations not applicable here). The Supreme Court normally didn't take cases unless the cases were significant (which this was not), or to resolve disputes among the lower courts. We didn't have that either; we had a decision against us but none for us. Ergo, no conflict.

In this case, our head of litigation had decided that the chances of getting the Supreme Court to review the case were too remote to pursue an appeal, and had decided not to even seek review. This led the two of us to have a shouting match that reverberated through the halls, where he told me that he "had never seen a case with a chance of success closer to zero than this one," and I responded that I thought he was wrong and in any event, "we couldn't afford not to appeal, given the money at stake."[48] We filed the appeal.

The Supreme Court not only took the case, but unanimously overruled the lower courts and held emphatically that the filed tariff doctrine was still very good law. Now the dominos fell in reverse order, as one after the other, the rest of the cases were wrapped up successfully.[49] Ultimately, though the reseller cases presented billions of dollars of exposure, we collected more in unpaid charges than we paid out in damages.

Tariffs were wonderful things. They not only protected AT&T from liability, but there were all sorts of other benefits that came from using tariffs because of the legal fictions that had grown up with the regulatory schemes in which tariffs played a central role. Two other rules

---

48   Our head of litigation, Mark Rosenblum, was a brilliant lawyer and is a friend. In fact, in addition to bailing me out of trouble here, he later retired and became a volunteer emergency medical technician, and helped save my life when in 2009 I had a severe heart attack while walking my dog!

49   There was one other case that we tried to completion, PSE v. AT&T. (The rest were either settled inexpensively or dismissed.) PSE had agreed to commercial arbitration, which meant that in exchange for getting a quick decision, we were able wrap several FCC complaints and their federal antitrust lawsuit into one proceeding. They were so used to winning at the FCC that they were shocked when the three-member arbitral panel ruled totally in AT&T's favor, giving us a judgment of twenty-seven million dollars in unpaid bills and dismissing all of their claims. They promptly filed in bankruptcy court so that we didn't collect anything, but it nonetheless was a sweet end to an ugly chapter.

in particular are worth mention: first, a customer is presumed conclusively to know the content of the tariff under which he is provided service. That means that no other notice other than a tariff filing is required to inform the customer of a change in their service, including a rate change. State consumer protection laws regarding things like informing consumers of rate increases didn't apply to us. Why? Because we filed tariffs setting out the new rates, and state laws were powerless to change what was in our tariffs. Add to this that we eventually won the right to make tariffs effective on one days' notice, and we could make a tariff filing that increased rates, filed after the close of business, effective at midnight. It didn't matter that AT&T literally had more than a hundred thousand pages of tariffs on file; all customers were legally presumed to know whether we had changed a comma!!

Adding to the carrier's arsenal was a second principle – repeatedly upheld by the Supreme Court -- that the tariff trumped everything else, including an explicit agreement between the carrier and the customer.[50] Even if the customer had a signed contract or had been promised a certain price, it was the tariff that governed. I had occasion to use this power in an unfortunate episode with MCI over service they had ordered under Contract Tariff No. 360.

Custom arrangements normally were open to other customers only for a short window of time, typically thirty days. After that, the custom offer was closed and could not be ordered. CT 360 was an old and poorly written tariff that not only gave aggressive rates but also had a free month of service in the eleventh month of each of three years! That may have made sense for the customer for whom the tariff was

---

50 There was a famous case involving the trucking industry, where it had become commonplace for carriers to offer discounts to customers not reflected in tariff filings. Decades later, and billions of dollars of discounts having been granted, the Supreme Court ruled that tariff charges must be collected, even in the face of explicit agreements to the contrary.

originally written but not MCI! The peculiar evil of this particular tariff was that there were no requirements that the usage of the free month relate in any way to the usage in the other eleven months. MCI could have given us no business in eleven months and then demanded that we carry all of their traffic one month each year, including paying their access bills. And that month would have been totally free, according to the tariff language.

This became an issue because an enterprising AT&T sales rep found the old tariff and filed it again in order to please a particular customer, without going through the correct processes of obtaining legal review of tariff filings. This filing re-opened the tariff to any customers who wanted it for a new thirty-day period. MCI had people whose job it was to read all AT&T filings; they spotted it and ordered the service. The matter escalated quickly to me, and I went down to talk to the FCC about the situation. The FCC was totally unsympathetic to us, which sadly was no surprise. I made no headway with the section of the FCC, the Common Carrier Bureau, which regulated AT&T, so I took matters into my own hands. We filed a tariff amendment limiting the free month to no more than the average usage of the other eleven. The FCC howled, MCI protested, but I was on solid ground, and they both knew it. I settled this matter for five million dollars in order to avoid having a very visible fight, though it was one I knew I would win, over AT&T's ability to change terms in a deal even after the deal started. This was not good news to our large customer base who employed expensive lawyers to negotiate individual deals with us, and who believed a deal is a deal.

Why any carrier with half a brain would want to get rid of tariffs is difficult to understand. Still, AT&T wanted this, for the simplistic reason that our competitors didn't have to file tariffs. For years, AT&T campaigned for an end to the unequal treatment. We were considered by the FCC to be a "dominant carrier" – the only long distance carrier considered to be dominant – and therefore were the only carrier required to file tariffs. No one stopped to think about the wonderful advantages a tariff world conferred on the carriers, at least not until we used the powers to extricate ourselves from trouble. Shortly after the CT 360 situation, the FCC ordered AT&T to stop filing tariffs, using our actions there as a basis for the new requirement. We had achieved our goal, misguided though it was.

The Patent Cases

The current legal framework for resolving patent disputes favors fakes. The whole reason why we have patents at all is to encourage real inventors who come up with useful ideas to publish those ideas in a form where others can learn about and practice those ideas. In exchange for that publication, in which the inventor is obliged to describe the invention, and explain how to use it, the inventor is given the exclusive right to practice his own idea for seventeen years.

The weakness in the system is caused by two phenomena: first, the patent office frequently awards patents when they should not, and second, many of those who file patent applications have no intention of trying to use the invention they create. Rather, they obtain patents with only one purpose in mind: to sue others they claim have been using the patent, even where the supposed violator was doing the same thing it is doing now before the patent was disclosed. Such lawsuits are frequently brought by people not in any business themselves other than the business of suing people. In other words, *they have nothing to lose.*

Why does the patent office make so many mistakes? It is true that Albert Einstein worked as a patent examiner in Switzerland, but not all who work in such places are Einsteins. It would take a legion of geniuses to catch those bent on using the system for extortion. Under the circumstances, and taking into account heavy workloads, one must conclude that patent offices do a reasonably good job. But it's not a perfect job.

AT&T was a natural target for such lawsuits. One lawsuit (Collins v. AT&T) focused on the architecture of AT&T's 5ESS switch, and requires an understanding of time-space-time digital multiplexing architectures to even understand what the case was about. The case was brought while I was still the lawyer for our switching systems business unit, and was filed in Midland-Odessa, Texas.

Now, patent cases are treated no differently by our legal system than slip and fall negligence cases. When one files a case and asks for a jury to resolve a very complicated patent dispute in Midland-Odessa, Texas, it isn't because plaintiff has done research and concluded that the jury pool there has the highest competency in engineering design. I am not being cynical and mean no disrespect to the good people of Midland-Odessa, but it is because plaintiff has concluded that the jury there likely will have little to no engineering knowledge whatsoever! All plaintiff would need to do is to wave a copy of the patent before the jury, with the official-looking seal and ribbons affixed by the U.S. Patent Office, and the jury almost certainly would conclude it is valid.

AT&T was sued by the estate of a small inventor who claimed that AT&T had copied his work in designing the 5ESS switch, which by then was the most widely used switch in the country. His widow testified, and the jury from Midland-Odessa was told by the attorneys for this heroic inventor that this huge corporation *from New York* had stolen his ideas.

I don't know how close Collins came to the ideas behind the 5ESS switch, but I am completely confident in asserting that the Labs designed the switch without looking for or using any ideas other than their own. The switch, I am told, was developed literally over a weekend in response to the threat from Northern Telecom, a Canadian company and AT&T's major competitor in the U.S. market. Though AT&T had pioneered digital switching technology, it had not immediately seen the need for it, believing the existing analog technology offered a superior sound quality. When the Bell Operating Companies, then still a part of AT&T, had threatened to buy the Northern Telecom switches in preference to the Western analog switches, the Labs was given the assignment of coming up with a digital switch of its own. The 5ESS was the result. Collins was one of those inventors who work in their garages, and then believe that big bad corporate America stole their inventions. I talked to the inventors of the 5ESS, and am convinced that he was wrong; the question is whether we could convince a jury of just plain folk from Midland-Odessa, that we had not. I was doubtful that we would prevail even before I learned about the "missing document."

AT&T, like many other big corporations, issues fine-sounding policy statements from on-high, which it then ceases to follow years later, without going back and altering the policy statements. We had such a policy statement, signed by the Chairman of AT&T, stating that whenever we introduced a new product, we would conduct a comprehensive right to use study that would investigate all relevant patents to see if the new product infringed any. We had done no such study here, nor in fact did we ever do such studies. Our patent law gurus had decided the policy was wrong and in fact created more exposure than anything else.[51] In the Collins case, both judge and plaintiffs refused to accept that we had not performed a right to use study. This was something, after all, that the Chairman had ordered be done with every new product. They assumed instead that we were hiding the study because it contained something about the Collins patent adverse to AT&T.

---

51 If a person knowingly uses a patent that he has no right to use, he is guilty of "willful infringement." If that is proven, the plaintiff is entitled to three times his proven damages. Our patent attorneys concluded that it is better not to look in an early application of "don't ask, don't tell," but didn't get around to changing the policy.

This was all explained to me at the eleventh hour by our patent attorneys who then inquired what I planned to do about it. Specifically, I was asked how I wanted to handle the hearing the judge had scheduled to investigate why he should not hold AT&T in contempt for willfully failing to turn over a document critical to the case. On my way to Midland-Odessa a few days later to appear before the judge, I passed through Dallas. Looking out the window from the terminal, the land was flat as far as the eye could see. It was the flattest place I'd ever seen. The person behind the counter asked where I was going. When I told her, she let the concept of Midland-Odessa percolate in her brain for a moment before volunteering, "Man, it's flat out there."

The hearing resulted in our being found in criminal contempt for which the judge proposed to fine AT&T. The case resulted in a judgment against AT&T in the amount of thirty-seven and a half million dollars. To encourage AT&T to settle, plaintiffs also asked in post-trial papers that the judge enter an immediate injunction against us continuing to violate their patent, pending appeal. Had the judge agreed, we would have had to abandon our appeal, or shut down the network. Fortunately, he did not.

Though the result was worse than I anticipated, I was not so naïve that I expected my view of "justice" to prevail. I had already prepared Dan Carroll (the head of our switching business unit) for a decision against us. I believed we had done nothing wrong, and therefore with a clear conscience recommended that we pursue our appeals to the patent court of appeals. We did and we prevailed completely, including even a reversal of the lower court's finding of contempt, on procedural grounds. We were lucky.

We didn't always win. We ended up litigating part of the way, and then paying for a license to a number of patents obtained by Ronald Katz. Katz was at least a very clever man. Whether he was evil or a genius in addition is something I don't profess to have an opinion about. What I can say factually is that he would attend Bell Labs forums open to the public and then file patent applications, and that he never attempted to put into practice any of the things he patented. Still, he obtained a large number of patents covering call distribution techniques used in call center equipment sold (and used) by AT&T. And finally, he sold his rights to sue AT&T to MCI.

I don't mean that he sold his patents. He didn't. What he sold was solely his rights to sue AT&T for using his patents without a license, and yes, you can apparently do that. MCI was more than happy to handle the lawsuit because it had a grudge to settle. MCI had only months before settled our case against it for violating the Weber patents for 800 service by agreeing to pay AT&T a hundred million dollars.[52]

In patent litigation there is something called a "Markman hearing" at which the judge determines the scope of the patent. The ruling is really a double-edged sword because, if read broadly, the patent covers more applications and is therefore more valuable, but it is also easier to invalidate. A court can invalidate patents even after being issued by the Patent Office if one demonstrates that "prior art" existed on some or all of the claims in the patent, but was not disclosed in the application. The broader the patent, the easier it is to demonstrate the existence of prior art. Katz's patents were given a very broad reading in the Markman hearing.

At this point, AT&T lost courage, and decided to settle. Part of it was because by the time the litigation had reached this point, Lucent had become independent and Mark Rosenblum (AT&T's litigation chief)

---

52   Roy Weber was an employee of Bell Labs when he came up with the idea for 800 service. AT&T obtained patents on the service and ultimately sued MCI for providing 800 service without a license.

had convinced Rich Rawson (Lucent General Counsel) that Lucent was responsible for two thirds of the settlement. MCI got its hundred million dollars back, though it was mostly at Lucent's expense.

The Right of Way Litigation

AT&T's long distance network was constructed using digital micro-wave technology, which AT&T had invented. It used radio transmission to carry the signals long distances, with near perfect quality due to its digital nature. While AT&T also used fiber optics as a transport technology (where lasers, invented by AT&T, would send signals down strands of glass fiber, also invented by AT&T), the majority of its long haul traffic was still transported by digital radio.

Then Sprint launched its pin-drop advertising campaign, extolling the virtues of an all-fiber network, and claiming that its network was superior to AT&T's because it was all fiber. It didn't matter that digital radio was as good as fiber for transporting voice traffic[53]; it mattered that Sprint was making headway convincing people that they would be better off if their calls traversed the country in fibers rather than through the air. This was intolerable to AT&T – under no circumstances could we accept a world where anyone had a network superior to our own. AT&T responded by making plans to deploy an all-fiber network itself.

The major problem with building a fiber network is that you physically need to lay cable over thousands of miles of routes. Under normal circumstances, it would take years to negotiate with the thousands and thousands of landowners involved. To solve the problem in this instance, AT&T turned to the railroads that had laid tracks across the

---

53 Atmospheric conditions could affect digital radio if very severe. On the other hand, fibers are vulnerable to cable cuts.

country in the 1800s and had presumably cobbled together the rights to run trains across their rights of way. The only problem was that the railroads didn't know exactly what rights they had and their records were in disastrous shape. For many stretches, the records simply didn't exist, and the railroads had no real interest in doing the work necessary to see what rights they had. Nor did AT&T have the time; Sprint had dropped a pin for crying out loud and AT&T had to build a fiber network! Now!!

The AT&T Network team was in such a rush that AT&T agreed that it would indemnify the railroads for any problems with the rights of way AT&T was buying from them. No, that is not a typo -- AT&T, the purchaser promised that if the rights of way that the railways were selling to it were insufficient, then AT&T would defend the railroads and pay any amounts to landowners that might have to be paid, on top of what we were paying the railroads for rights they didn't have!

As soon as the backhoes began digging trenches to bury the cable, lawsuits from landowners began pouring in. It turned out in many cases that while the railroad had the right to run a train through someone's back yard, it had no right (because of the nature of the language in the easement it had obtained originally), to bury a telephone cable by the tracks. Once AT&T did enough work to approximate its liability, it began settling with the landowners. Ironically, between the amounts recovered by AT&T from its insurance carriers and the reductions in payments to the railroads – due to more careful inspection of our right-of-way contracts that would not have occurred absent the litigation – AT&T actually came out ahead financially as a result of this litigation, even after all the payments to the land-owners.

e. Plaintiff's Litigation

Most corporations view litigation with disdain, and are reluctant to initiate litigation themselves. Litigation frequently produces imperfect results, and should not be viewed as the first option to resolve disputes. But it is a waste of corporate assets to forego litigation that has a reasonable chance of success without some legitimate reason. Perhaps it was the fact that I was a "plaintiff's lawyer" for the first few years of my career, but during my tenure, AT&T too became more aggressive in pursuing legal redress when other means were ineffective.

In most cases, we had a specific business goal in mind that we gladly cashed in the litigation to obtain. We sued Lockheed Martin when one of our communications satellites they were to place in orbit for us blew up along with their rocket during the attempt. We wouldn't have sued about that, but they compounded our problems by refusing to give us an early launch slot for its replacement. Timely launch slots are as valuable as the satellites themselves. We had committed to our customers to be ready for Olympics coverage, and being late was unacceptable. Lockheed was unyielding until we sued, but became more reasonable after we had done so.

We also sued News Corp. after that company reneged on a contract to give us their business exclusively. The contract was clear, but they kept making up reasons why they were giving almost all of their business to MCI. We had a brief exchange of letters, and then I brought suit a few days prior to the end of the calendar year, which was also their fiscal year. The case was sufficiently strong that I knew they would need to affect their end of the year results through establishment of a reserve to cover their potential exposure.[54] I guessed correctly that this was

---

54 Proper accounting requires companies to establish reserves to cover the expected liability in lawsuits they are likely to lose.

not something they would want to do, and that it would shine a light on their purchasing manager (who I was told by our sales team was buying from the pretty MCI sales rep for the wrong sorts of reasons.) In any event, News Corp settled and we dropped the lawsuit for a new one hundred and fifty million dollar exclusive contract.

By far the most fun I had with litigation was the racketeering case we brought against MCI. It started when our fraud team detected unusually high spikes of long distance calls coming from Canada. Normally, the traffic flows between the two countries are relatively balanced, and for that reason, AT&T and the leading Canadian telephone companies had agreed to a zero accounting rate. That meant that for calls originating in Canada and terminating in the U.S., the Canadian companies would bill the customer and keep the full price, and AT&T would absorb its internal costs and pay the terminating access for them. Similarly, for calls from the U.S. to Canada, we would bill the customer and keep the full amount, making no payments to them.

This worked well if the traffic was balanced, which is why the sharp increase in south-bound traffic was a concern. Our fraud people, working with sales and Dave Ritchie, one of my attorneys, soon figured it out. MCI had struck a deal with at least one of the Canadian companies and was hauling U.S.-to-U.S. traffic to Canada from where the calls were being handed off to AT&T for completion as if the calls had originated in Canada. Because access charges were applied both on the originating and terminating ends of a call, this had the effect of making AT&T pay the terminating access charges for the MCI traffic. And since these calls appeared to AT&T as if they were originating in Canada, AT&T had not been collecting anything for them. This scheme allowed MCI to win at least one large customer – Wells Fargo Bank. The day after MCI started carrying Wells Fargo traffic, MCI began diverting the bank's traffic and running it through Canada. In other words, a call from a branch bank in New York to the bank's headquarters in California would be routed to Canada first, and then handed off to AT&T as if the call had originated in Canada. AT&T would then deliver the call in California, paying the local company terminating access to do so. AT&T would be out its own network costs plus the costs of access, and would receive no revenue from the call. MCI would save the costs of transporting the call plus the terminating access, less whatever it paid the Canadian company for participating in the scheme.

By far the largest hurdle to suing MCI under the Racketeering and Corrupt Practices Act (RICO) was to convince skeptics within AT&T that we had a case. Most were unfamiliar with RICO, and thought it was applicable only for hard-core criminal activities, not things like misrepresenting the origins of traffic. Given how poorly the RICO statute is written, it is woefully underutilized. If one can demonstrate two or more related criminal actions in furtherance of a common scheme, which can include fraud using the mails or telephone, then one can satisfy the jurisdictional requirements of the statute. Once "in," the statute also confers broad discovery rights. And it gets better. If one prevails, the statute also provides that your damages are trebled as a matter of law, plus the plaintiff's attorneys' fees are paid by the defendant.

Here, I believed that we had MCI on repeated instances of fraud, but it didn't really matter. Plaintiff's litigation should be played like hockey; in hockey, the right tactic is often to dump the puck in the opponent's zone, and then see if you can dig the puck up and score. In litigation, so long as you have something when you file, you don't have to have everything. MCI was such a dirty company (in my opinion) that it was a reasonable assumption that AT&T would find all sorts of goodies when we started going through their files.

MCI's defense followed a familiar course. Their initial denials gave way to a statement that they had a right to do what they were doing. However, behind the scenes, they contacted our general counsel at the time, Jim Cicconi, to see what it would take to settle the case.[55] Jim asked me to put together a wish list of things we might want from MCI, and I supplied him one that would have been worth about a quarter billion dollars to AT&T. He told me that I was shooting too low, although we ended up settling for less, the case being yet another victim of MCI's bankruptcy filing.

Before MCI's bankruptcy filing, there was an air of indifference to MCI's behavior. AT&T publicly identified Wells Fargo as the customer whose traffic was being re-routed. Wells Fargo's response was that they didn't care what MCI did so long as they got a lower price. The Wall Street Journal attacked AT&T, not MCI, questioning our motives in bringing the case. This was their response to our giving the story to the New York Times rather than the Journal[56], but even so, it felt as if once again, MCI had been the bad boy who got away with murder.

---

55 Cicconi was (and still is as of the date of this writing) a consummate lobbyist, first and foremost. When John Zeglis left his post as General Counsel to become the President of AT&T, Jim added AT&T's legal affairs to his position as the company's chief lobbyist. He was the only senior executive of AT&T to survive the acquisition of the company by SBC in 2005, and became the senior lobbyist for the combined company, relinquishing the legal affairs, which had never been his true love.

56 The Journal had sniffed out the story first, and approached AT&T on a Friday asking what if anything we were doing to prepare a case against MCI. AT&T played dumb. Then, on Saturday, we leaked the story to the New York Times that we would be filing on Monday the RICO case against MCI, and the Times ran the story on Sunday (a day when the Journal didn't publish). I was told that we were unhappy with historical coverage by the Journal that someone at AT&T thought unfair. Here, we made it look like the Times had scooped the Journal, and the Journal's coverage of the incident was negative towards AT&T in the Journal thereafter.

That changed with their bankruptcy filing, which at the time was the largest bankruptcy filing in U.S. corporate history. The bankruptcy filing almost didn't happen. MCI was seeking to merge with Sprint, the third largest long-distance company at the time. The deal had already cleared all U.S. regulatory clearances, when the European Commission, which had a much lesser interest in a merger of two U.S. companies, nonetheless stepped in and blocked the merger on grounds that it could harm competition in Europe! (Each of them had small presences in Europe, which the EC used as a hook to claim that competition there would be lessened if the two combined!) That action brought down the house of cards at MCI WorldCom.

WorldCom had a history of taking over companies, sometimes larger than itself, using stock for the acquisition so that it could do what was called a "Pooling of interest" transaction under the accounting rules then in effect. Such transactions permitted the participants to write off unlimited amounts of good will without a charge to earnings. Essentially, WorldCom was able to cleanse its books of a lot of accounting mischief after each transaction and start over. It had counted on doing the same thing with Sprint. When the transaction was halted by the EC, however, WorldCom was forced to disclose that it had major, major problems with its accounting. In addition to the bankruptcy filing, it subsequently had to admit to criminal wrongdoing and its CEO, Bernie Ebbers, went to jail.

There was one major plaintiff's case that we lost. We sued the government, more specifically the General Services Administration, for failing to give us business that we thought we had won in connection with the government network, FTS 2000. The GSA did a wonderful job of taking the government's needs for telecom services and putting the entire package out for bid. FTS 2000 was a ten-year contract, with a secondary price competition in year seven.. In other words, the original two winners government (AT&T and Sprint) were invited to resubmit bids for the last three years. The bid documents stated that the low bidder would get an increased share of the business. AT&T priced very, very aggressively to get the additional business and won the re-bid. However, AT&T didn't get the additional business. After being giving the run-around for much too long, we brought suit --- and lost! The court ruled that the government didn't have to honor its offer, and could give us as much, or as little, business as it wanted. The court pointed to the fact that the bid terms were for an "indefinite quantity" of business, and stated that under the law we could not file a claim based on not being given the business we expected.

If that is the law, it shouldn't be. Either the GSA should have given the extra business to AT&T, or alternatively, they should have been required to disgorge the extra discount. The Court in allowing them to keep the discount without giving us the bargained-for extra business rewarded the government for behaving unethically.

Chapter 18

The Telecom Act of 1996

By the mid-1990s, the situation was as follows: the RBOCs had gotten the right to make and sell equipment[57], but the prize – to enter
the long distance market – still eluded them. Judge Greene was an
ardent believer in this aspect of the MFJ. And, for the time being,
AT&T still had enough raw political power to block their attempts
to have Congress overturn the MFJ. There was little doubt, however,
that it was a question of when they would overcome the opposition
in Congress, not whether. They simply had too much money to lose a
political fight where money served as the ammunition. Judge Greene
also was getting older and was already on senior status. He could be
counted on to stick to the restrictions on the RBOCs entering the long
distance market, but how long would it be before he wasn't around
anymore? AT&T faced a dilemma: the walls keeping the RBOCs out
would eventually come down, and if AT&T had not come up with
a solution to the access problem by the time they did, it would not
survive.

Ironically, those who had fought to prosecute the case against AT&T,
like William Baxter, exited the policy debate. Having accomplished
the dramatic dismemberment of AT&T, they now withdrew from the
debate concerning whether it had been a good idea. AT&T, which
had fought tooth and nail to avoid the MFJ, was now the only party
to support its continuation.

---

57   This relief was granted them by Judge Greene, who retained the right to
make changes in the decree.

AT&T was still a very powerful company, but one cannot continue to transfer billions of dollars every year to one's competitors without the relative strengths of the players being affected. The access charge regime colored all of AT&T's strategic thinking about future competition with the RBOCs. We would not have feared such competition on a "fair" basis, but there was little chance of that. AT&T had to pay a substantial portion of its revenues to the local companies, a significant expense that those companies did not incur themselves.

AT&T General Counsel John Zeglis decided to roll the dice rather than await the inevitable. AT&T did an about-face on legislation, and no longer opposed RBOC entry into the long distance market. Instead, the company proposed a checklist of terms that the RBOCs would have to meet as a condition of entry. The RBOCs bought into the idea of legislation as well, making it inevitable that something would pass if only the parties could agree on its terms.

The final terms imposed a fourteen-point checklist the RBOCs had to meet on a state-by-state basis before being allowed to offer long distance service. The checklist was intended to level the playing field so that AT&T and others could compete with the RBOCs. Among the many provisions was one that was key to creating the level playing field: access charges were to be "cost-based," and to the extent a subsidy was necessary to support local service, that subsidy was to be collected *through a separate charge* in a *competitively neutral manner*.

In addition to setting the conditions for RBOC entry into long distance, the Act also preempted all state laws limiting or prohibiting competition in local services. Before the Act's passage, every state had passed laws making competition for local services illegal. Similarly, the states had also made competition for intraLATA long distance unlawful.[58] All of these restrictions were now voided by Congress, which had the power to do it owing to the supremacy of federal over state laws.

Congress also required the RBOCs to allow two types of competition, in addition to facilities-based competition: (1) competitors, if they wished, could sell the RBOCs' end-to-end services as a pure reseller, consistent with the FCC's long standing policies favoring such competition. But the act also unveiled a new concept, (2) requiring the RBOC's to unbundle their networks into the different piece parts (such as switching, the loop, etc.) and so that competitors could buy only what they needed. That way, if a carrier like AT&T had its own switches and wanted to use them, it wouldn't have to pay the RBOC's for duplicative switching. These piece parts were called "unbundled network elements."

The best part of the statutory scheme for competition based on unbundled network elements was the economics – the pricing of the network elements was set by the Act at long-run incremental cost. In addition, if a competitor won the customer in this manner, that company became the customer's access provider as well, and was entitled to collect the access revenues from other carriers delivering traffic to the customer. Finally, the FCC initially interpreted the Act to mean that a competitor could order the "platform" – i.e., all of the elements bundled together into a working service and the same rules would apply.

By opening up the local markets to competition, the Act (as initially interpreted by the FCC) required the RBOCs to do cost studies so that when a competitor handed off a local (as opposed to a long distance call), the participating local companies would have a cost-based charge

---

58 The MFJ had set up Local Access and Transport Areas (LATAs), larger than the typical local exchange area, where the RBOCs could provide service.

to charge each other. This was called "Reciprocal Compensation." *The cost studies ultimately resulted in a charge of approximately a tenth of a cent.* The tasks done by a local company to complete a local call were identical to what it would do to complete a long distance call! The costs to the local company were unaffected by how far the call might have traveled before being handed off to the local company for completion. Yet, the local company charged a tenth of a cent to handle the local call, and ten or twenty times that amount to handle the long distance call.

The language of the statute seemed very favorable and AT&T was optimistic – in the beginning. Indeed, the initial interpretations of the new Communications Act of the FCC were positive and AT&T embarked on an all out effort to enter the local market, depending upon unbundled network elements as a means of entry. It was the RBOCs that were on the defensive, refusing to acquiesce to the FCC interpretations and dragging their feet on implementation.

Two things intervened to sink AT&T's future as a local provider, however. First, the RBOCs appealed the FCC decisions to an appellate court in the Mid-West that was hostile to the FCC and other "Washington, D.C. bureaucrats." Second, Reed Hundt retired as FCC Chairman and with Bush's ascendancy to the Presidency of the United States, Bush appointed (in January 2001) Michael Powell the next Chairman of the FCC.

With the benefit of 20-20 hindsight, I believe that the RBOCs' appellate strategy was better than AT&T's. They appealed the FCC order interpreting the Act to the U.S. Court of Appeals for the Eighth Circuit in St. Louis, Missouri, rather than the D.C. Circuit, which hears the majority of appeals from the FCC. It was a shrewd decision, as the court overturned most of the FCC's pro-competitive policies. The Eighth Circuit was then overturned by the U.S. Supreme Court, but this whole process took so much time that the original order was never implemented before Powell became chairman of the FCC, and began backing off the agency's earlier pro-competitive positions.

And AT&T? We had done very well overall in the FCC order, but had lost one key point: the FCC gave a loose and unhelpful interpretation of the standard that access charges be cost based, stripping it of real meaning by stating that this only meant that the charges relate in some way to costs. We should have filed an immediate appeal, but we didn't. The FCC pleaded with AT&T not to file an appeal, but instead to intervene in favor of the FCC Order. Their concern was that if we came out swinging and attacked their order as well, then it would appear that the industry was solidly aligned against the FCC. AT&T intervened in the appeal in favor of the FCC order, in the hopes of protecting the unbundled network elements section of the order. It was a gamble, and it backfired. When Powell later gutted the network element provisions of the original order, we were left without a clear appellate shot at the access issue.[59]

Powell had originally been put on the five-person FCC by President Clinton to fill one of the Republican seats. Powell, a registered Republican lobbyist, was better known for being the son of Colin Powell than as a communications lawyer. To the extent he was known at all, it was in the broadcast rather than common carrier arena. The battles he fought had to do with decency standards, including what to do with the network for allowing Janet Jackson's unclothed breast to be televised during the half-time show of Superbowl XXXVIII.[60]

---

59 It is unclear whether we could have gotten the case to the Fifth Circuit, but that Court had very favorable language on the access issue. We would have had to file immediately and then hoped for the best.

60 The fleeting exposure of one of her breasts due to a "wardrobe malfunction" drew a record $550,000 fine for CBS, a fine subsequently vacated by the U.S. Court of Appeals.

When George Bush was elected President in 2000, he was able to create a majority Republican Commission. As part of doing so, Bush nominated Powell to be the next Chairman of the agency. Perhaps AT&T could have blocked his confirmation had we wanted, but at the time (2001), our lobbyists in Washington didn't seem to think he would be as bad for the company as he turned out to be.

The trap was closing in on AT&T. It faced a decisive disadvantage because of access, and its hopes to enter the local market were becoming dimmer with Powell calling the shots at the FCC. It was in this dire situation that AT&T set out to find a new Chairman. Bob Allen was ready to step down, and the Company needed a strong leader if it were to survive.

Chapter 19

A Good Leader Is Hard To Find!

Robert Allen had been neither a terrible chairman for AT&T, nor a great one. During his tenure, AT&T did rectify the mistake it had made by giving its wireless licenses to the RBOCs. It bought McCaw, the largest non-Bell provider of cell service. But Allen was relatively conservative in re-positioning the company in ways necessary for it to prosper long-term. Perhaps at another time Allen would have been an ideal chairman, but the time required bold action. Allen was more thoughtful than bold.

Allen was born in 1935, and therefore was not at mandatory retirement age in 1996, when the search for his successor began. He let it be known that he intended to stay on for a year or so after the CEO-designate was hired. This decision, which should have been but was not overruled by the AT&T Board, eliminated most of the top candidates from consideration. (It would have been unusual for a Board to challenge a decision by its Chief Executive Officer; Boards for the most part went along with what management wanted to do.) Here, however, AT&T was in trouble, and few truly talented CEO-types, who likely were already "number ones" somewhere else, wanted to come to AT&T to be a "number two" for an indefinite period.

Both Allen and the Board became active in looking for a successor. Allen didn't have a natural successor internally, so the search shifted outside the company.[61] As difficult as it might have been to find the right person, the person ultimately chosen was clearly not him!

John Walters had been the CEO of J.R. Donnelly when he agreed to become AT&T's President, and the presumptive heir to Bob Allen. He had no relevant telecom experience unless you count Donnelly's printing of yellow page directories as participating in the phone business. AT&T was a high technology business, heavily regulated, and (as I hope you've come to realize) complex. Donnelly was a printing business, which was not regulated at all. Nor did Walters have a proven track record of success that would have made him stand out from the crowd. He was affable, and by all reports, a good golfer. That apparently was enough to get his foot in the door.

While at AT&T, he seemed to impress no one. According to those who worked closely with him, Walters often appeared disinterested even in the most critical matters affecting the company. His seven-month tenure coincided with the first merger talks between SBC and AT&T. Lou Chakrin, a senior executive of AT&T, had been giving a briefing to Walters in the office of retired executive Vic Pelsen. Walters didn't ask questions during the briefing. Instead, his attention seemed drawn more to the numerous, personal mementos that had been acquired by Pelsen during his career. The mementos were still there waiting to be packed and shipped to Pelsen. Walters walked around the room,

---

61   Given the importance of having a strong and talented CEO, the absence of any real succession plan was inexcusable. The person who at one point had been considered the prime internal candidate, Randy Tobias, left AT&T to become CEO of Ely Lilly in 1993. He had been vice-chairman of AT&T from 1988-93. President George Bush appointed him to an ambassador level position in 2003, as this country's representative to the international fight against AIDS. Publicly, he supported abstinence rather than condoms as being the right approach to fight the disease. In 2006, he was put in charge of all foreign aid. He resigned in 2007 after it was disclosed in the press that he was having call girls come to his apartment in Washington D.C.

looking at them, and then began picking some of them up, and putting them into his pockets. When the briefing was over, Walters thanked Chakrin, and left the office, his pants sagging from the weight of the things he had taken.

On another occasion, the company's lobbyists had lined Walters up for a press conference in Washington D.C. to lay out the company's position on access charges. The press conference started, but Walters did not appear. Those representing the company did what they could to placate the reporters, while frantically trying to locate him. He finally appeared after a number of reporters had already left, and won none of the remaining attendees over by giving as his excuse that he had been unavoidably detained because of a meeting he had had with the builder of the mansion he was constructing in New Jersey.

While he was at AT&T, rumors began circulating that Walters had attention deficit disorder. Hal Burlingame, the head of the Human Resources organization within the company, met with Walters to make him aware of the rumors. Burlingame then asked him how he could help. Walter's response was to demand that Burlingame be fired and his organization be audited. The audit, which uncovered nothing amiss, was conducted while Allen and the Board decided what to do.

Seven months after he joined AT&T, the AT&T Board informed Walters that he would not be promoted to CEO. One member of the Board told the press that Walters "lacked the intellectual leadership" to run the company. Walters resigned. The Board's decision not to elevate Walters to the chairmanship may have saved the company even greater heartache in the future, but it also cost the company a severance payment of twenty-six million dollars immediately. It also was very public and made both Allen and the Board look foolish, triggering reports of a "management crisis" at AT&T. The Board pushed Allen to the side, and took over the search for the next Chairman, eliminating in the process Allen's previous determination to stay on even after the "chairman-designate" was hired.

Enter C. Michael Armstrong. If it took a rocket scientist to run the company, he was your man. Actually, he wasn't really a scientist, but he had been the CEO of Hughes, an aerospace company. He also had been involved, according to many reports, in attempting to sell satellite technology that had military significance to the Chinese government, while advocating changes to U.S. government policy (shifting licensing authority for sensitive exports from the State to the Commerce Department) that would have made it easier to obtain licenses for future satellite technology export.[62]

Notwithstanding the baggage, Armstrong looked and sounded like a CEO should. He talked tough in a deep voice, had a disarming smile, and rode a Harley for fun. Had central casting been looking for someone to play a CEO, I can think of no one better. He was charismatic, and won the hearts and minds of the Wall Street Journal and others whose jobs were to tell the public about the goings-on at AT&T.

In the first bloom of Armstrong's tenure, AT&T's stock soared to record heights as "the Street" concluded that AT&T had finally found its man. Looking at things from the outside, he appeared dynamic, buying both Teleport Communications Group ("TCG") for $11.3 billion dollars and IBM's Global Network for another $5 billion dollars. Fortune magazine's take was typical: "...AT&T's chances look far better than they did a year ago. In three months Armstrong has transformed AT&T from a tired also-ran to the telecom "it" company."

---

62 Commerce looks at things typically from an economic standpoint, and believes its mission is best served by promoting export. The State Department takes a broader perspective, and is more likely to block exports of sensitive technology on the grounds of political concerns.

Even several years after he had done to the company what I will describe below, the popular sentiment outside the company was that if Armstrong couldn't walk on water, he came awfully close. Oprah Winfrey loved him: "If he were running for President, he is one of the few people I have ever known for whom I would quit my job and personally campaign. He's a leader with guts, vision, and the balls to back it up." Business Week continued with its own accolade, concluding, "But AT&T is a company that has been in decline for a long time. It may be that someone with Armstrong's talents has arrived too late to achieve more than a modest victory."

Talents? Guts? Vision? How easily people are duped! Armstrong was a terrible leader, and a sucker for fast talking salesmen with bridges to sell. It is clearly true that the company was in a terrible trap because of the access charge situation, but it still had resources to bring to bear to change that, as witnessed by the fact that Armstrong himself spent about a hundred and fifty billion dollars trying to remake the company. His problem was his own limitless arrogance, and an enduring belief that whatever he didn't understand wasn't important.

Let's look at what really happened.

Fortune magazine was right that there was an air of hope and anticipation when Armstrong came. Every single officer, indeed every single employee, wanted him to succeed. All of the approximately two hundred officers of the company were gathered for a dinner, and Armstrong was introduced. Putting his stamp on things immediately, he announced that there would be no bonuses for officers that year because our "customer satisfaction scores" were unacceptable.

There were two problems with that statement, as I later corroborated with Hal Burlingame, the head of AT&T Human Resources at the time. First, the scores were not terrible; in fact we had made the original targets. Armstrong had made that part up because it suited the end he wished to achieve. Second, he failed to mention that one officer would get a bonus – him! He had a personnel contract without the contingencies that affected the rest of us.

After that Armstrong went on to talk about the business, and made the point that the company needed to hire a new head of our international operations. In fact, AT&T had just done so. Armstrong was told this but didn't blink, responding, "Well, I mean to be his boss!" Mark Baker, a talented executive who we had just hired from British Telecom, learned in this manner that he would not be given the job for which he had been hired, and quickly left the company. His departure came just as AT&T began negotiations to merge much of our international operations with those of British Telecom, an endeavor in which Baker's background and experience would have been invaluable.

Those who worked with Armstrong the most were the first to become disillusioned. Officers began sharing their feelings of disappointment, and began leaving in droves. John Zeglis told me that he tried to warn the AT&T Board about what was going on but they didn't listen. Zeglis became demoralized, and began planning his own exit. Gail McGovern, an extraordinarily popular executive and head of our consumer business left, as did her number two, Dan Shulman. Jeff Weitzen, the head of AT&T's business services unit, left. Many of those who left were tremendously talented executives who left because they no longer had faith in the direction the company was being taken.

I remember being at a Consumer Leadership review with Armstrong shortly after he arrived. Gail was going through the financial numbers when Armstrong interrupted, and told a story about how he had a neighbor who had just learned that he, Armstrong, was now the CEO of AT&T, and that his neighbor was quite annoyed at receiving telemarketing calls from AT&T in the evening. Having promised his neighbor to look into it, Armstrong demanded to know why such calls were placed in the evening rather than earlier in the day when, according to the neighbor, they would be less intrusive.

Most of those in attendance felt the sudden need to look down at their papers, pick up pens and pencils that had just been knocked off their desks, or frankly do anything other than look at Armstrong. Finally, Gail cleared her throat and responded, "Because that's when they're home."

Her answer, based on years' experience of bloody telemarketing wars with MCI, didn't satisfy Armstrong who ordered the practice stopped immediately. At the next review, the data showed a drop in market share. Armstrong, sounding not at all pleased, asked why. The answer was that the hit rates on telemarketing had fallen because of the change in time when the calls were made. Armstrong looked puzzled. Someone explained that they had moved the time when they called from evening to afternoon and the percentage of people that they were getting to answer the phone was significantly lower. Armstrong looked exasperated, as he directed the thickheaded team to move the calls to the evening!

Armstrong clearly thought of business as a man's world, and this may have factored into the lack of confidence he showed for McGovern. I base this on two different incidents. The first was his comment to his executive assistant, repeated for several of us, that upon returning from a luncheon honoring the woman at AT&T who had done the most for the business that year, Armstrong cracked, "If you book me for that next year you better allow more time." As he said that, he used his hands to mimic someone talking without stopping.

The second incident occurred after he left AT&T. A good friend of mine, a woman and fellow officer, went to Armstrong to ask for a reference. She had worked at AT&T for more than twenty years, and had been a successful executive. As they talked, she mentioned that after years of effort, she and her husband had adopted a child. Armstrong asked how old the child was, and she informed him that the child was two. Armstrong refused the reference, stating that he didn't believe women should work outside the home until the children are five years old.

Perhaps Armstrong as a man can best be described by focusing on his reaction to the centerpiece of corporate culture when he arrived, a credo that had been developed to reflect, and further shape, the values of employees. It was called the "Common Bond." It was a noble set of values that most in the company tried to live up to, with values such as Integrity, Respect for the Individual, and Teamwork. Started under Allen's tenure, it could have been naïve and overdone, but it wasn't. In fact, in an industry buffeted by quick-buck artists and scoundrels of every kind, it set AT&T apart, and was a big part of the reason AT&T didn't follow others down the paths of crooked accounting and flim-flam books. The Common Bond was the Company's Ten Commandments and was celebrated in publications, in forums attended by all senior management, and was painted on the walls at company headquarters.

Armstrong didn't like it, and ordered that all evidence of it be removed (except in one place where it would have cost too much to remove). He had the walls on which it appeared painted over, and it was dropped from all company communications without discussion or comment. It was simply gone.

Other insights into Armstrong's character can be gathered from other stories. Bill Hannigan, who had been the CEO of Saber, a large private telecom network operator before joining AT&T as the head of Business Services in 2003, told me the following: Sabre had issued a request for proposal to telecom companies to furnish a large amount of transport requirements needed by Sabre to fill out its network. AT&T was competing for the business, and one day Hannigan got a call from Mike Armstrong, the new CEO of AT&T. Hannigan expected the usual stuff on such calls like, "My door's always open to you if you have issues with us," and so forth. Instead, he was surprised when Armstrong began berating AT&T's current performance, saying that he knew AT&T stunk at operating networks and at customer care at present, but committing that he, Mike Armstrong, was committed to turning things around and once he did, AT&T would provide the best service in the industry!

Like most other customers, Hannigan thought that AT&T already was the performance leader in the industry; the question was whether its prices were competitive. Hannigan told me that he was frankly shocked at the fact that here he was considering AT&T and its CEO calls him up to tell him that AT&T's services had major problems! Hannigan ended up picking AT&T, not because of Armstrong's call but in spite of it. To him, the call was one of pure egotistical arrogance by someone who didn't know his company's service capabilities.

Armstrong's inflated view of himself could be confirmed by that wonderful source of information and company gossip: the AT&T executive drivers. AT&T maintained a fleet of cars, and had about a dozen drivers whose jobs were to drive officers where they needed to go. Until they knew you, the drivers would sit mum. They would listen of course, and given the constant use of cell phones in the car, frequently were privy to highly sensitive information. As they became more familiar with you, they would occasionally ask questions about things they had heard about the company. If they grew to trust you, they would speak, not about the things that the company was doing, but about the personalities and quirks of those they drove.

Armstrong was a favorite topic of conversation. One of the stories was about his daily commute to work. Armstrong had a home in Connecticut where he frequently stayed. When he did, he would take the company helicopter from a heliport near his home to the company headquarters in Bedminster, New Jersey. The only unusual part of the arrangement was how he covered the few miles from his home to the heliport. Armstrong had certain drivers he favored, and would not let the others drive him. One of the "favored" drivers lived in Pennsylvania. According to several former drivers, Armstrong insisted that he be driven the short distance between home and heliport by a company driver, rather than take a taxi or drive himself. To avoid any risk that he might hit traffic and keep the Chairman waiting, the driver would either come up the night before, or leave his house literally in the middle of the night, *i.e.*, between 3 and 4 a.m., to take him to the heliport. Then the driver would drive the one to two hours to company headquarters to be available should the Chairman want to go anywhere else.

Armstrong was a caricature of a Chairman, whose determination to be decisive turned out to be fatal to the company. He refused to take the time to listen or learn, leaping from deal to deal without looking. True, much of what I have collected are anecdotes about the man. But the theme of arrogance appears too often to be accidental.

For those who might say that they don't care about his qualities as a person so long as he was good at leading a company, I've got more bad news. Armstrong proved to be a total disaster as a CEO, judged solely by his record! He spent about one hundred and fifty billion dollars buying various companies and businesses. Not a single deal worked, and the cumulative effect of the deals was to lose approximately seventy billion dollars, give or take, *plus* to so weaken AT&T's traditional business as to make it impossible for it to survive. Some of the deals were so inane that you're going to think me untruthful as you read the descriptions. Unfortunately, they were every bit as ugly as described.

Chapter 20

At Least We Didn't Buy the Brooklyn Bridge.
Say, How Much Is That Bridge, Anyway?

Michael Armstrong was Chairman of AT&T from 1997 – 2002. During that period, he made acquisition after acquisition. Not a single one came close to meeting its stated objectives. The one common theme in all of them was that AT&T grossly overpaid for what it bought, with the full support each time of its Board and investment bankers, and then failed to even attempt to use the assets it acquired in the manner intended!

In 1998, AT&T paid $11.3 billion dollars for Teleport Communications Group ("TCG"). TCG was a competitive local exchange carrier who claimed to own a number of fiber rings in metropolitan markets.[63] It had revenues of only about five hundred million dollars, *and had never made a profit.* During due diligence, two AT&T attorneys stumbled across the fact that TCG didn't own any of its fiber rings – they were owned by its cable company shareholders, and leased to TCG for 99 years. Generally, businesses only think months ahead, so no one seemed to mind very much what would happen in 99 years when the leases expired. But not owning your own facilities becomes problematic when you want to upgrade, modernize or extend the facilities. Still,

---

63 Fiber rings were the access vehicles of choice for large corporate customers, not only because of their capacity to handle large amounts of traffic, but also because they offered redundancy. For any customer on a ring, there were always two directions a call could be routed and still reach the customer. This offered protection for their businesses from cable cuts, which are all too frequent.

rings with complications were better than no rings at all. What was particularly toxic about the transaction was the price.

To pay more than eleven billion dollars for a company that had never made a profit, and had no realistic prospects of ever making one, was – to say the least -- unwise. Moreover, much of TCG's revenues weren't retail revenues paid by willing customers; they were, instead, access charges paid by AT&T and other long distance carriers or reciprocal compensation paid it by local exchange carriers. Both of these revenue streams were temporary phenomenon due to regulatory quirks, and were going to disappear over time no matter how well TCG was managed.

TCG was what AT&T called a "high cost CLEC." Such companies would frequently charge more than the cost of the retail call to originate or terminate calls for long distance companies. (AT&T might charge its own customers a nickel a minute for the call, and would have to pay thirteen cents for TCG's end of the call. If TCG had both the calling and called customers, then AT&T would pay TCG twenty-six cents for the call.) TCG would do whatever possible to stimulate calling, including paying colleges a percentage of the take to sign up their students, and setting up "bridges" for "chat-lines" where customers, mostly young, would call in to talk to other callers, oblivious to the fact that each minute they were on, TCG would charge some unlucky carrier more than that carrier charged its own customer for the service. When a young girl was raped by someone she had met on a TCG chat line, the New York State Public Services Commission ordered TCG to provide a blocking feature so that parents who didn't want to permit their children to call such numbers could block calls from their homes. TCG never complied, and AT&T inherited the disaster, and a twenty-seven million dollar proposed penalty by the state commission. AT&T worked out a settlement that cost it considerably less, but this was not the sort of business that one paid more than twenty times revenues to obtain!

Gelding Goliath

Given AT&T's exposure to high access charges and the public embarrassment of owning a company who was a high-cost CLEC, AT&T had no choice but to begin shutting down TCG's access operations.

Worse than its revenue problems were its back office processes. They didn't exist, or at least not to the level used by AT&T. Sure, AT&T would have installation or billing issues – it had tens of millions of customers and some of its systems were old and needed to be updated. But at least it had systems. TCG didn't. It had customers it could count in the thousands, not millions, yet provisioning each new customer was an adventure. TCG would try to overwhelm problems with bodies because it hadn't developed the systems necessary to be efficient.

Armstrong knew none of this. He hadn't asked and didn't seem to care. He was so impressed by Bob Annunziata, the Chairman of TCG and a fast-talking salesman, that he put him in charge of all of Business Service once the acquisition was complete. Annunziata lasted three months and then quit.

Annunziata was a charismatic and aggressive salesman. He had worked at AT&T in sales but had topped out as a "third level" and had left to find his fortune elsewhere.[64] He was a charming man, and a good leader in some respects; but the basic blocking and tackling of business wasn't his strength. I was the chief lawyer for Business Services, and when he became the leader of that unit, I became his lawyer. We had a number of interactions in group meetings, but it was my first smaller meeting with him that left an impression. He asked Barb Peda and me to join him in his office. Barb was a good friend, and a very talented businesswoman. She led our wholesale business, a tricky business because it sold to competitors of our retail operations (such as Bell

---

64 In AT&T's hierarchy, there were five levels of management before officer, and then three levels of officers.

South). She also had the 900 service business, and it turned out that was what Annunziata wanted to talk about.

As mentioned earlier (Chapter 17, *supra*), 900 service had been seized upon by service providers who wanted to offer services such as gambling, what the state attorneys general in many states considered pornography, and fortune telling. Service providers loved the service because it provided a billing capability that was unique. From AT&T's perspective, and it should have been a great way to capitalize on its billing capabilities. It cost AT&T very little to bill for 900 service. It required merely another line on the customer bill; the cost of generating the bill itself, the envelope and postage were already being absorbed by the customer's telephone service. It therefore was practical to offer service even for small amounts of money. And in many states, it was lawful to restrict a customer's regular phone service for failure to pay any portion of the bill, including 900 service.

Unfortunately, it was a constant challenge to preserve the useful aspects of the service while keeping under control those who would tarnish our reputation or involve us in litigation.[65] In 2004, AT&T filed an application to discontinue the service, which after delays caused by opposition from unhappy service providers, was finally granted.

---

65 Christmastime was peak season for the 900 industry. I remember being involved two Christmases in a row on internal conference calls with Jeff Weitzen (then the head of Business Services) and the irate sales vice president who had our largest 900 service provider accounts. (Ironically, the sales vice president was the same person who some years earlier had been the uncooperative network director with the unlimited budget in the southern region I mentioned earlier. See Chapter 9, *supra*.) Her customer was running misleading programs, which one of my attorneys had stopped. She became so irate at "AT&T's overly conservative lawyers" that she twice escalated the dispute to Weitzen. Both years, he listened to her complaint, my response, and sided with me.

We sat down in Annunziata's office. He was casually dressed, his open shirt revealing a substantial gold chain he wore around his neck. He asked me about the guidelines we had for 900 service providers, and I began to explain what they were. He cut me off, saying he knew what they were, adding that he didn't like the fact that we refused to run programs with explicit sexual content! I mentioned that the reason why we didn't wasn't because we were prudish, but for a very sound business reason – we had been threatened by over twenty states with criminal prosecution before we added the prohibition to our guidelines. He didn't care, and told me that we had crossed that bridge when we bought a cable company. While I tried to figure out what he meant, he stood up, and ended the meeting, telling me to figure out how to do what he wanted, which was to open the service to providers who wanted a vehicle to sell pornography. His exact words were, "That's why we have lawyers."

I didn't agree that helping Annunziata get AT&T into the porn business was why AT&T employed me. I did nothing to further his request, and fortunately was spared further confrontation about this by his departure three months later. Because the acts he wanted to pursue were considered criminal acts by many of the states, it is a confrontation I was comfortable I would win, though not without significant risk to my job.

The next story was told me by Michael Keith, who both preceded and succeeded Annunziata as the head of Business Services.[66] Armstrong had ordered Business Services to add five hundred new sales people

---

66 In the roughly ten years I was chief counsel to the unit, there were eight different leaders of Business Services. They were John Petrillo, Gail McGovern, Jeff Weitzen, Michael Keith, Bob Annunziata, Michael Keith (part 2), Dave Dorman, Rick Roscitt, and Betsy Bernard. Bill Hannigan assumed the job while I was still at AT&T, but during my last year I worked on a special project, and my successor (Elaine McHale) became his attorney.

whose job it was to sell the local services the acquisition of TCG made possible. All of the new sales people were at a training session, and Annunziata was supposed to give a kick-off address to fire them up for the sales campaign. He made no efforts to prepare anything. Ten minutes before he was supposed to speak, he leaned over and asked Michael Keith, who was now his subordinate, to give the talk instead. Keith had planned only to make a toast at lunch, which Annunziata said he would do. Annunziata's toast was his standard one, "Do it to them before they do it to you," amusing the first few times you heard it but less than satisfying when you realized that this was all he had to say.

TCG did have some value, but it was nowhere near the $11.3 billion dollars that AT&T paid. Demonstrating why one should never invest based on what you read in the financial press, Fortune magazine concluded, "The move was so impressive that even AT&T's closest competitors had to congratulate him. Says one, 'I think it's a terrific strategy.'" The assets were fine; but starting a pattern that affected every transaction Armstrong did, they were worth only a fraction of what AT&T paid.

Michael Keith resumed the top job in Business Services when Annunziata left, though it was clear that Keith was not Armstrong's kind of guy. Michael knew the business, but was quiet and thoughtful, without the sort of braggadocio that Armstrong liked. All Keith did was deliver the numbers. In 1999, by jettisoning every expense that wasn't carved in stone, and investing virtually nothing back in the business that didn't have immediate payback, Business Services made six billion dollars. That wasn't enough to fuel the purchases Armstrong wished to make. The six billion target having been met, Armstrong lifted the target to nine billion dollars. AT&T's dangerously inept Chief Financial Officer Dan Somers had calculated the target by applying MCI's reported margins to AT&T's revenue stream.

When Keith objected, saying that you couldn't trust the MCI numbers, Somers accused him of making excuses to cover his inadequate performance.

Armstrong was just getting started. In June of 1998, AT&T bought the nation's largest cable company, TCI, for $48 billion dollars. The price equaled about four thousand dollars per subscriber and was the highest price paid for any cable property to that point. After trying unsuccessfully to negotiate contractual arrangements with other cable companies to provide access for AT&T services, Armstrong bought Media One in March 1999 for $54 billion dollars or nearly *nine thousand dollars per subscriber*, after winning a bidding war for it with Comcast. AT&T was now the largest cable operator in the country, at a cost of approximately one hundred and five billion dollars. There was virtually no due diligence done in either case; in Somer's words, you don't do due diligence when you are doing something strategic!

The price tag for the business was only the beginning of the trail of wasted billions Armstrong left in his wake. Armstrong was so inattentive to "details" that John Malone was able to burden AT&T's new cable operations with an unbelievable contract between AT&T and Starz Encore, a programming entity controlled by Liberty Media, a Malone company. Under that contract, AT&T was obligated to pay Starz on the basis of how many of its customers were *offered* the service, rather than the standard in the industry of how many customers actually took the service. This translated to costs to AT&T per actual Starz subscriber of thirteen dollars per year, nearly double the industry average of seven dollars per year. Not only that, but AT&T agreed to cover two thirds of any cost overruns beyond what Starz had originally projected it would cost to buy programming, and that exposure was uncapped!

Under the contract, AT&T faced losses of about three hundred million dollars for each of the next twenty-one years! Armstrong didn't just overlook the terms once, but twice!! As Forbes magazine reported in September 2001, "Remarkably, in June 2000, Armstrong expanded the Starz contract to include Media One subscribers when it bought Media One." Ignoring the buying power the status of the largest cable company gave it, AT&T ended up paying almost double what the smaller companies paid for programming. Armstrong had a CEO voice, but his business judgment at times was abysmal!

John Malone, the CEO of TCI, had hired Leo Hindrey as his chief operating officer in 1997, and Armstrong wanted Hindrey to run AT&T's cable business. Malone had given Hindrey a contract with a rich severance provision; Armstrong made it richer. Armstrong's original organizational design was to make Zeglis the consumer head, and have Hindrey report to him, aligning the interests of the two units. But Hindrey refused to report to Zeglis, and Armstrong so badly wanted Hindrey that he agreed. Hindrey reported directly to Armstrong. Though the whole purpose of spending the hundred billion dollars for the cable companies had been to help AT&T's consumer business, yet there was a total lack of cooperation between the two groups from that point on due to the schism of leadership.

In many ways, Hindrey was an effective manager. He streamlined TCI's operations by selling systems that were "out of footprint," that is, outlying systems geographically. At AT&T, however, he never fit in, and he lasted less than a year. It was what he said publicly rather than what he did as a manager that hastened his departure. Armstrong, while still trying to romance the other cable companies, held secret talks with AOL, a company viewed by the cable industry as an enemy. Hindrey went public and denied the talks had occurred, which was untrue. Because the talks could have had an impact on the share prices of a number of companies, Jim Cicconi had little alternative (given AT&T's exposure under the securities laws) but to correct the public record, and told Hindrey in advance that the company would do so.[67] Hindrey argued against this, saying it would make him look either like a liar, or like he didn't know what was going on within his own area of responsibility. The correction was made nonetheless, as it had to be.

Hindrey, if not a liar, was not a mindless adherent to the truth. He told listeners how he had overcome a childhood filled with adversity, and about how he had left home at age thirteen and worked in the Merchant Marine. He would even embellish the tale with the name of the ship on which he worked. None of this was true. His mother and other siblings reported that he had an uneventful childhood, and worked for his brother following his graduation from high school!

Hindrey could have weathered these episodes of being untruthful; he was unable, however, to weather Armstrong's reaction when he told the truth. In September 1999. Hindrey was openly critical of Armstrong at an investor meeting. Hindrey left the business shortly thereafter, submitting his resignation, which was accepted. He didn't go away empty-handed, however. In addition to two years salary ($1.8 million), and an undisclosed bonus, he was also given a million shares of AT&T stock. At the trading price of approximately forty dollars a share, this brought the value of his package to about forty-five million dollars. That's not bad for working for AT&T a little less than a year.

Why did Armstrong agree to such a rich severance package? Presumably, he did it for the same reasons he over-paid for the systems themselves: Armstrong was convinced that he had to have Hindrey, as he did the systems, and when he was in that state of mind, his sense of value

---

67 AT&T's policy was not to comment either way on any material discussions. Not only do disclosures such as made by Hindrey have to be accurate when made, but they also bring with them the added obligation to update the investing public should the status of such discussions change.

went out the door. His disdain for the internal AT&T managers led him to think that he needed someone from the outside to manage this prized asset. Who better than the man who was running TCI for John Malone?

After he left AT&T, Hindrey became active in Democratic Party politics. Do you remember former Iowa Senator Tom Daschle, who was nominated by President Obama to be Secretary of Health and Human Services? If so, you may also remember that Daschle withdrew his name from consideration following disclosure by the press that he had accepted limousine services from a wealthy donor worth many thousands of dollars without reporting it or paying taxes on it. The donor's name? You guessed it: Leo Hindrey, putting some of the money from AT&T to work.[68]

It was only after the cable deals were done that Armstrong was able to convince Chuck Noski to come join him at AT&T as the Chief Financial Officer. He had tried unsuccessfully to recruit Noski earlier from Hughes, where the two had worked together. In this case, I agree with Armstrong completely in his assessment of the man. Noski was quiet, but a brilliant CFO who, had he come earlier, would have added the financial discipline to the mix that could have made all the difference in the world. While all of Armstrong's purchases weakened AT&T (because they all involved expenditures well in excess of the value obtained), the transaction that really pushed a teetering company over the edge was Media One. AT&T simply couldn't afford the price it paid. While this is speculative, I cannot believe that Noski – based on my observations of the man – would have supported this transaction.

---

68 Daschle had reportedly promised Hindrey the top position at the Commerce Department before he withdrew.

In the numerous meetings I attended with Noski, I was always struck by the fact that he not only asked the right questions, but he listened to the answers before making his decisions. He was the total opposite from Dan Somers, AT&T's Chief Financial Officer during the company's buying binge, who fancied himself a deal maker. The problem was that the deals done with Somers leading on finance were unmitigated disasters, because Somers lacked the patience and attention to detail to do better.

I worked directly with Somers only on two deals: the "Unitel" deal in Canada, and the formation of our joint venture with British Telecom. The Canadian deal involved the establishment of a competitive carrier north of the border, run by AT&T but with several Canadian partners and British Telecom involved as minority partners. What made the deal a disaster for AT&T was a provision, agreed to by Somers, requiring us to buy out the Canadian partners under such generous terms that it cost AT&T about five billion dollars to buy their positions in a venture that never turned a profit.

The BT venture, as described earlier was also a financial disaster for AT&T. We took our international operations, or at least those that served large business customers, operations that had always been profitable, and mixed them with BT's similar operations in such a way that somehow, the mix lost about three quarters of a billion dollars the first year. I remember a specific incident that in my mind characterized Somer's approach to things. One of the last issues we had with BT was an arcane tax issue that I won't attempt to explain. What our tax experts told me was that AT&T would save about fifty million dollars if we infused our capital into the venture in a certain way. BT, based on its similar mysterious tax advice from its experts, didn't like that way of proceeding, which posed some forgettable risks to it.

This was not the sort of issue I understood well enough to resolve, not being a tax lawyer myself, nor was I willing to simply walk away from fifty million dollars. I put it on a list of issues that were teed up for resolution by the CFO's of the two companies. It was a Sunday afternoon when the two men had their telephone call. Somers called me afterwards and told me to write the section of the provision on capital infusion the way BT wanted. I asked him what had happened on the call and why he had given them the point. His response was that he "wasn't about to risk something "strategic" for fifty million bucks."

The AT&T landscape during Somer's tenure as the company's Chief Financial Officer was littered with lost billions wasted in pursuit of something "strategic." AT&T inherited TCI's 23% stake in Excite@ Home when it purchased TCI. It paid another $2.3 billion dollars to increase its share position to 38% and its share of voting rights to 79%. Reported bickering between Hindrey and Armstrong as to what Excite@Home should do strategically left it doing nothing in particular, and on October 1, 2001, nearly out of funds, the company filed for bankruptcy protection.

In August, 2000, AT&T invested $1.2 billion dollars for a 32% stake in Net2Phone, an Internet telephone company owned by IDT Telecom, a Newark-based company. In the second quarter of 2001, less than a year later, AT&T reduced the value of its investment on its books by $1.1 billion dollars, and later that year sold it back to IDT for about one hundred million dollars.

Meanwhile, Armstrong was laying off tens of thousands of employees in order to cut costs in the traditional business so that he could build a war chest to fund his purchases. The problem was that the cuts were too deep: there was not that kind of fat in the traditional organization; there had been so many lay-offs that AT&T in fact was as lean or leaner, with lower overheads, than its competitors at this point.

It isn't easy making a billion dollars. Especially in telecom where margins were paper-thin and falling, and people were being told to do more with less, a billion dollars was tough to make. Employee morale was in the toilet because the employees felt (correctly) that Armstrong didn't appreciate or understand what they were doing, and because they saw him buying things that lost their value so rapidly following their acquisition by AT&T.

The cumulative effect of Armstrong's deal-making finally hit home in May 2000. AT&T issued public announcements that month, advising the public that it would not make the profit targets Armstrong had promised previously that it would. The stock lost more than ten percent of its value the first day, but that was only the beginning. Before the tailspin was over, AT&T had to do a reverse 5-to-1 split (where an owner of five shares would be issued one new share) in order to keep AT&T's share price above a dollar!

As AT&T's share price continued to plummet, the predictable law suits were filed against the company, claiming that AT&T knew it would have no chance of making the numbers Armstrong had claimed it would, and that it should have disclosed this much earlier. In truth, the problems of Business Services were *knowable*. The reason why an earlier disclosure wasn't made was that Armstrong refused to accept what he was being told; he confused his belief in himself (and the fact that he had ordered the unit to make more money) with reality (that the unit was out of gas and could not).

The failure to find a competent successor to Bob Allen was AT&T's fourth Colossal Failure. If one compares the company before and after Michael Armstrong, one realizes what a disaster he was as Chairman. There is no question that AT&T needed to escape the access –charge trap it was in. Armstrong, however, frittered away tens of billions of dollars, breaking the financial backbone of the company on purchases that accomplished little or nothing. AT&T spent more than one hundred and five billion dollars on Armstrong's two cable investments, selling both for fifty-three billion a few years later; bought IBM's global network and TCG, paying more than fifteen billion dollars for the two, neither of which ever turned a profit; lost another one billion plus on Net2Phone; lost another five billion on Unitel; and last but not least, lost another three point two billion on Excite@Home. *Every single investment made by Armstrong was a disaster, with total losses exceeding more than seventy billion dollars! And, to gain the war chest necessary for his purchases, Armstrong starved AT&T's long distance business of resources, leaving it with little hope for long-term survival.*

Armstrong was not the type to go down with the ship. Or even admit defeat. Not when he could (drum roll please)… restructure the Company!

Chapter 21

Corporate Fission, or How Investment Bankers Make Money Once Their Victims Are Too Broke to Buy Anything Else

There are two ways to look at what AT&T did from, say, May 2000, when it disclosed its disappointing results and its share price headed for the basement, to October of that same year, when Armstrong announced he was going to "restructure" the company by breaking it into little pieces: the first is that Noski, who realized quickly that AT&T would not be able to pay off the debt it had amassed, did what he thought necessary to save the company; or second, that Armstrong believed the investment bankers who started urging him to break up the company in order to "unlock shareholder value."

Both are correct. Noski knew, with Business Services on track to miss its plan, and with the stock plummeting to single digits from over sixty dollars a share, that the company had little room to maneuver. It would have to sell assets.

As for Armstrong, he didn't even pause before changing from someone who had been preaching that the way to win customers was to bundle everything customers would want, to someone who now said that bundling was unimportant and that it would "unlock shareholder value" to split the company apart. Dick Martin, the head of AT&T Public Relations and in my view a public relations genius, came up with the slogan "the next logical step" to describe what was, in truth, a complete reversal of strategy.

Remember "synergies?" Synergies represent all those additional revenues and/or cost savings that result when you put related businesses together. That was the whole reason why AT&T had spent over one hundred billion dollars buying cable systems. AT&T didn't buy them to enter the cable business on a stand-alone basis. It did so because it wanted to own its own facilities all the way to the customer and thus avoid the more than ten billion dollars in access charges it still was paying each year. The cable systems were supposed to provide a facilities-based solution allowing AT&T to offer local service, long distance service, Internet access and cable service all on its own facilities. Far from being the next logical step, the only reason to break AT&T apart having paid such a huge premium to put the capabilities together was because AT&T couldn't service the debt it assumed to make the purchases.

AT&T's bankers stopped talking about synergies and started talking about "unlocking shareholder value." Synergies are only available if you have the money to buy things, and AT&T no longer did. On the other hand, if two businesses have no real synergies between them and there are circumstances causing the combined operation to be valued less than the operations would be if separated, then theoretically, it might make sense to unlock the shareholder value by separating them. Best of all from the perspective of the investment bankers, you don't need any money at all to participate; whereas you have to buy something to get your synergies, you have to sell to unlock shareholder value. So Armstrong, the same devious, sniveling investment bankers at his elbow,[69] set about breaking the business into four parts: AT&T Broadband, meaning our cable operations; AT&T Wireless; AT&T Consumer Services; and AT&T Business Services.

---

69 My talents as a writer are far too limited to do the investment bankers true justice. The only author who comes readily to mind who could describe these vultures in a way that comes even close to capturing their evil character is Charles Dickens. Think of Uriah Heep on steroids and you begin to understand their essence!

While synergies do exist but are hard to achieve, unlocked shareholder value rarely exists and in the case of AT&T clearly did not. The proposal to separate the business and consumer businesses, for example, overlooked that the two businesses were naturally complementary. Networks are sized for peak call loads, which are driven by business demand and occur naturally enough during business hours. One of the problems to be solved then was to load the network with traffic at nights and on weekends to avoid having the capacity sitting idle. Because that is when most consumer calls are made, the incremental network costs for the consumer traffic is close to zero.

Not only would these efficiencies have been lost, but there were other very real costs that would have been incurred if you separated business and consumer operations into two entities. Each unit normally accounted for its use of the AT&T network by taking an internal book charge. This was an accounting entry so that AT&T could monitor the profitability of each unit. However, the supply of network capacity to the units was not a taxable event because the units were all part of the same taxable entity. If they were to be separated legally into different legal entities, the use of the network by the consumer business, or by the wireless or by broadband entities (assuming as had been planned that the network would stay with Business Services) would have been a sale of service from one taxable entity to another, to which state sales tax would apply. Nor was this a small change; think about sales tax on five or ten billion dollars times the relevant state tax rates. On five billion dollars times the NJ tax rate of seven percent, the extra costs associated with this unlocking of shareholder value would have been $350 million dollars a year.

In fact, the consumer spin-off never occurred, nor did the spin of AT&T Broadband. The next chairman (Dave Dorman) stopped the spin of Consumer Services because it didn't make business sense. The Broadband spin was preempted by an unsolicited bid for AT&T's cable interests by Comcast. The bid was presented on July 1, 2001, and was for $44.5 billion dollars of Comcast stock. AT&T's board had a fiduciary obligation to consider the offer in the interest of its shareholders, as an alternative to the plan to spin the same business to shareholders. The Board ultimately decided a sale to a third party was preferable, and asked for those interested to submit best and final offers in December of 2001. Comcast upped its offer slightly, to $29.2 billion dollars in cash, and the assumption of $24 billion dollars in AT&T debt, for a total of around $53 billion dollars.

In two years, AT&T's cable investments had lost half their value. The systems had not collapsed; revenues were up about ten percent per year. The reason why the value appeared to deteriorate was because the original prices paid by AT&T for its cable systems were much higher than was reasonable. If the reason why Armstrong paid such an exorbitant price was to use the cable facilities to help AT&T's consumer business by deploying AT&T's own facilities to customers, then there is no answer to the question: why then didn't AT&T attempt to do so? The plain truth is that AT&T never used the assets it bought for their intended purpose. It may have begun to offer local service in isolated circumstances, but there was no major, national offer of local service using the cable facilities while AT&T had them! Armstrong spent a hundred billion dollars, had two years to do something, anything, and never did!

This was the place where a true leader would have done what was necessary to make certain that the company collectively got behind the effort to use the cable franchise, together with its telephone offerings and its brand assets, to do battle with the RBOCs. The answer to the question of what sort of leader Armstrong really was, sadly, was that he made no real effort to do so.

Of course, if you try to justify the purchases on synergies, then it goes without saying that there was no corporate value to unlock by separating the two. The two units either were worth more together (synergies) or more apart (unlocked value). They cannot be both.

Wireless was spun-off to shareholders as originally intended, and Zeglis went with the business to be its Chairman.[70] It was still called AT&T Wireless, because AT&T had agreed as part of the spin to license the brand to it. This caused great friction as AT&T subsequently threatened to pull the brand on the ground that AT&T Wireless was hurting the brand by offering poor service. This issue so inflamed Zeglis that he threatened to shift AT&T Wireless's considerable long distance demand from AT&T to a different carrier.[71] This was averted at the last minute by the efforts of the officer assigned to mentor the AT&T Wireless-AT&T relationship: me!

Under the circumstances, the spin of AT&T's wireless business into an independent company might have been necessary to save the wireless division. It desperately needed capital to expand and improve its network, and AT&T (the parent) was in such horrible shape that its ability to raise capital was severely compromised. In fact, NTT Do-Ko-Mo, a large Japanese company, was willing to invest about five billion in AT&T's wireless business but only after it was assured that its investment would be in wireless only.

---

70 AT&T shifted several billion dollars in debt to the new company, and sold additional shares to the public in the new company. This enabled AT&T to reduce somewhat the debt it had accumulated.

71 Wireless companies provide substantial quantities of long distance services to their customers. They rarely build their own long distance networks, choosing instead to buy wholesale long distance service from long distance companies and package it with their own service under their brand. AT&T Wireless bought from AT&T and was in fact our single largest customer. We didn't always treat them that way.

On the other hand, the spin-off of its wireless business was the death-knell for what was left of AT&T. Wireless was clearly the future for telecommunications, and to dispose of it in order to reduce AT&T debt, from AT&T's perspective, was like a drowning man selling his life preserver in order to afford swim lessons. It all depended on one's vantage point: if you were going with the wireless or cable assets, then the elimination of the wounded telephone business was a blessing in disguise. It was only if you were sticking with Ma Bell (like me and the few hundred thousand remaining AT&T employees) that one would wonder why these assets, so necessary to any chance AT&T had to survive, were being given away.

And what about Armstrong? He had insisted that he become chairman of the merged Comcast/AT&T cable businesses. Comcast agreed and made him the CEO for one year. He had a very fancy office in New York City, but nothing to do. The Roberts family controlled enough shares to control the board, and wanted no part of Armstrong. In fact, Armstrong was probably the only person involved in those discussions that may have believed he would have a substantive job to do. At the end of the year, he left.

Armstrong's plan to split the company was dressed up as a restructuring. In reality, his actions had so injured AT&T that it had little chance to survive, and *the plan was his attempt, having sucked the traditional business dry, to jettison it.* The people of AT&T who had worked their lives to make the company great deserved better than that. Armstrong was more arrogant than intelligent; sadly, the company paid the price because AT&T's Board could not tell the difference.

Imagine instead that an enlightened CEO of AT&T had come in and spent fifty billion dollars on wireless, building up rather than disposing of this part of the business! AT&T today likely would be the dominant wireless company in the country, and in a world moving in that direction, would have been strongly positioned for the future. Hey, wait a second! Did I mention that wireless traffic doesn't pay access charges? But that would mean that this was an alternative to the cable adventures! Hmmm, why didn't Armstrong think of that?

Chapter 22

Dave Dorman Comes to Town

Dave Dorman was a telephone man. He had worked for Pacific Telephone and Southwestern Bell before he was hired to head our joint venture with British Telecom ("Concert"). When that venture failed, he was brought into AT&T as head of Business Services. Concert had a strong central staff, including a highly regarded attorney from AT&T who had been its general counsel. It was by no means certain, therefore, that Dorman would want me as his chief lawyer at Business Services. To the contrary, all the reports reaching me were that he (1) was extremely happy with the legal support he had had at Concert; and (2) was miffed at some of the positions I had taken restricting Concert's ability to sell in the U.S. market (as opposed to the international market), which, as I read the formative contracts, was not within its purview.[72]

These were not rumors from unknown sources. In fact, the Concert general counsel visited me in my office, and told me both things before sharing the news that he had already talked to Dorman and was going to get my job. His mistake was that he thought that his relationship with Dorman was so tight that he next went after Jim Cicconi, my boss and the AT&T general counsel. Cicconi was far more astute and politically connected within AT&T than was I, and easily outmaneuvered him. When the dust cleared, the Concert general counsel left AT&T and I became Dorman's lawyer in Business Services.

---

72 Since I had personally negotiated the agreements, I spoke with some authority concerning what they meant.

Dorman and I developed a strong working relationship while I was his lawyer, which paid dividends for me when Armstrong left and he became chairman. Professionally, I was able to score some key successes that brought in, or kept, several hundred million dollars of revenue. In addition to the litigation that resulted in a huge new contract with NewsCorp, I also parachuted into a negotiation at the last minute at Dorman's request where we were about to lose a very large west-coast client to MCI. The customer was steaming mad at us, and with good reason. I looked at the ten issues that the prior negotiating team had been unable to resolve, and in my first meeting with the customer gave them six of them without asking for anything in return.[73] The mood completely changed, and the customer's attorney had to break to try to gain control over his clients, who despite his best efforts, were determined to be equally generous. Timing is everything, and after negotiating around the clock for four days, I was done. I flew back to New Jersey, arriving just in time to attend a meeting of the Business Services leadership team. Ken Sichau, our head of sales, was in the middle of his presentation, when Dorman saw me walk in.

"Well?" he asked.

"We signed last night," I answered with a big smile. I was given a round of applause. It doesn't get better than that. Or does it? Dorman gave

---

73   One of my favorite issues was the applicable interest rate to be charged if payments were late. We obtained services from the bank so they knew when we were the buyer we would not agree to anything greater than 6% late fees. On the other hand, as a seller, we insisted on 18% annual interest. Apparently, due to weaknesses in our biller, we could only bill 18%; we could not bill higher or lower, and we would routinely get stuck on this issue in contract negotiations! What made it possible for me to crack these issues was that the petty champions of our ridiculous positions knew that I would challenge them in front of Dorman if they didn't change their tunes. I called the VP who was in charge of late payments (among other things), told him he was being ridiculous, and asked if he wanted to explain to Dorman how this issue cost us a major account. Then I told the customer we would agree to the same interest rate in both directions.

me access to him, which is an invaluable tool. By access I mean that he would take my calls, or if he couldn't, would call me right back when he was free. Cicconi, my boss wasn't comfortable with the fact that Dorman would ask me to give my views directly to him on certain matters, even though I always copied Cicconi on my responses. He asked me not to do that but to funnel things through him. I so advised Dorman, who responded that he expected me to give him answers when he asked, and if Cicconi didn't like it, I shouldn't make Jim aware that I was doing it!

I was circumspect, because I was never certain of my footing with Dorman. I suspected at times that he might enjoy tweaking Cicconi by sharing something I had told him that Jim would know came from me. Nonetheless, the access to him was invaluable. On one occasion, I had been negotiating a settlement of our disputes with a high-cost local exchange provider, one who had been gouging us on access charges. We had been negotiating a deal for several weeks, when I learned that the FCC was going to come out the next day with a decision adverse to AT&T. Comparing what I had negotiated to the FCC order, my deal was seventeen million dollars better for AT&T. It wasn't enough money to solve world hunger but it was enough so that Ben Lamontagne, our access Vice President, was anxious to see what we could do to try to get them to sign that day.

I called the company's general counsel up, and asked if he knew that an FCC decision was expected imminently. The company he represented was located in California, and therefore might not follow events in D.C. as closely as we did. He had heard, however. On the other hand, he also thought (incorrectly) that AT&T could influence the FCC, and was anxious to sign a deal before the FCC order was released. The only hold-up was that he had a former governor of California on his board, and the man wanted to talk to Dorman before they would sign. I sent Dorman an urgent message saying asking him to please call the governor that day, stating that the call was worth seventeen million dollars. He called the governor, and we signed the deal that afternoon.

Another time, I got a frantic call from two wonderful friends (Eric Alexander and Emil Michael) I had met while negotiating a deal with their upstart company, Tellme. Tellme was a Silicon Valley start-up that had morphed into a top-notch voice recognition company. Barb Peda, our head of AT&T's wholesale business, wanted to sell them billions of minutes of 800 service in exchange for a piece of their company. She had good judgment, so when she asked for help, I jumped in. The sticking point was that Alexander and Michael were so brash that they were offending the team from Consumer Services who controlled our call centers that Tellme wanted to help automate using voice recognition technology.

I sized up the two negotiating positions, and then took Alexander and Michael out of the room. I told them that they were blowing it, and that if they wanted a deal they had to make the following concessions, listing less onerous terms than the Consumer folks were asking. Their one question was whether the Consumer team would agree, and I said yes. Next, I took the Consumer team out of the room, told them that *they* were blowing it, and told them what to ask for. Their one question was whether Tellme would accept it. Again I said yes. Not trusting either of them to summarize the deal without provoking the other, I laid out my compromise. Both parties agreed, and AT&T and Tellme started a very successful collaboration.

We encountered a difficulty a year or so later because Tellme's business had changed and they no longer needed the billions and billions of inbound (800 service) they had bought from us. We were reluctant to buy them back, and they made noises about selling them to American Airlines. That brought howls of protest from our sales team, since Tellme could afford to provide the minutes very cheaply. I called

Alexander and Michael, and told them if they sold the minutes to an existing AT&T customer, I would have no choice but to sue them. Michael, who had a Stanford law degree though he didn't practice asked a good theoretical question: "On what basis?" he demanded.

"I'll think of something," I answered. Alexander was the first to laugh, but he also got the message. The good news is that they not only pulled back from that sale, but also took my advice and found a company AT&T presently didn't have as a customer.

They called me some months later with the news that they were making good progress selling their platform to SBC (Southwestern Bell), AT&T's most significant competitor. If the sale went through, SBC would also need billions of minutes of 800 service, because at the time they did not have their own interLATA capabilities due to the MFJ. Not surprisingly, at lower levels within SBC, there was reluctance to use AT&T. We were implacable opponents politically and competitors in the market. Michael called for help, asking if there were any way I could get Dorman to call Ed Whitacre, the chairman of SBC to support the sale.

Once again I sent a message to Dorman, telling him that we had a chance to sell billions of minutes to SBC and that he should call me if he was interested. He was. I don't know what he told Whitacre, but Tellme got their call center business, and AT&T became the underlying 800 service provider. Jim Cicconi started his next weekly leadership call by telling me to keep my eyes open, because he had heard from Dorman that the Chairman had just sold billions of minutes to SBC, and he didn't want anything to go wrong with the contract. I promised him I'd do my best.

The problem was that these were small victories and a greater defeat was looming. Armstrong had not solved the access charge dilemma, and AT&T was still vulnerable to RBOC competition as soon as they met the standards for entry under the Telecom Act of 1996. For the first three years after the new statutory framework was in place, AT&T defeated each attempt by the RBOCs to demonstrate compliance with the 14-point check-list that the RBOCs were obligated to meet on a state by state basis. Then Verizon's application to begin providing long distance service was approved in New York in December 1999, and after that the battle was lost; once one state had approved entry, the rest soon followed. And unlike Armstrong, Dorman had no war chest to buy his way out of the trap.

Dave Dorman was for me a breath of fresh air. He was not universally popular, but I had no complaints. He treated me well, intervening with Cicconi to make certain my ranking and compensation put me in the top tier of lawyers. He was someone I wasn't afraid to joke around with. Best of all, he helped get things done.

It is interesting to speculate whether Dorman would have been able to save AT&T had he become chairman instead of Armstrong in 1997. I believe the answer is "yes," for the reason that he didn't share Armstrong's glaring weaknesses: Dorman already knew the business better than most, but was willing to listen and embrace good ideas, whether or not they were his own. Armstrong was so self-assured that he felt his decisions were the best and didn't look for help. At the very least, I would have expected Dorman to avoid the catastrophic transactions Armstrong did – the spin off of AT&T Wireless and the purchase for obscene prices of TCI, Media One and TCG.

Chapter 23

Power Lines: My Last Hurrah

In 2003, I met with Hossein Eslambolchi, a brilliant man and head of our Labs and Network groups. AT&T had maintained a small group of scientists even after spinning off Bell Labs with Lucent, calling the new group "AT&T Labs." It was tiny compared to the old Bell Labs, but I found the people creative and extremely competent. My goal for the meeting was to review with Hossein the different technological alternatives to reach customers without using the local loops owned by the local telephone companies. I assumed I knew about the various alternatives such as wireless or cable facilities. Still, I had asked Hossein for a comprehensive review to make certain I understood access technologies from a to z. Under the statutory scheme, if there were a practical alternative for us to use, then we lost the right to obtain access to the RBOC facilities at a wholesale rate. Thus, at the very least I wanted to understand what the RBOCs would argue.

We began working through a think binder of technical options Hossein's staff had put together. When we reached "Power Lines," I asked Hossein what that entailed. He explained that technology had been developed, partly by the Labs and partly by other companies, enabling the transmission of voice and data over power lines. This was news to me, and I assumed that it must be something that they were working on. I asked him when they thought that they would be able to determine whether or not this worked.

Hossein smiled and asked if I wanted to try it.

We walked back into a Labs building where I met the man in charge of the project. He gave me a tutorial on the different ways they were thinking of architecting the service, and then asked me to call anyone I wanted. I called my daughter who was four at the time, and asked her how I sounded. She laughed, and replied, "The same as usual, dad!" I told her that I would talk to her later, and then turned to my host, asking whether the call I had just made in fact had been over power lines. He smiled and told me yes. They had a working prototype, using a power line that they had running through the lab. I didn't really get excited, though, until later that day when I started going over the economics. Even using first generation electronics, this was dirt cheap, and appeared to have a cost advantage over both cable and traditional telco new builds. This was by no means a slam dunk, but it appeared far more capable than anything else in our arsenal. I asked whom they were working with internally. The response, "Consumer Services," caused me concern. Had it been within Business Services I could have influenced it to move more quickly. I had little confidence in our Consumer group; they were hemorrhaging share to both the RBOCs and cable companies, and seemed incapable of a response. I also had little confidence in the leadership team assembled by John Palumbo, a friend of Dorman's, who he had brought in to head the unit.

The power line project was a good example of the Consumer leadership malaise. The project had not been prioritized; instead it was lumped in with a half dozen other ideas that were being considered. They had copious vu-graph presentations, but the actual time frame for implementation was hopeless. The consumer plan was to do a limited market trial in two years, with the move into the market with a power line platform in three years at the earliest.

We didn't have that much time! In fact, the consumer timetable guaranteed failure by bringing everything along too slowly to make a difference. After trying without success to get the Consumer team more focused on the power line opportunity, I called Eslambolchi once more to do a sanity check on my own enthusiasm. He reiterated his view that this is the one technology that AT&T had in its arsenal that seemed ready to deploy. That was all I needed to hear. I asked to have a private meeting with the Chairman. Dave Dorman. He was as usual booked until the cows were scheduled to come home. Fortunately, I had earned enough points with his secretary Marie that when I said it was important, she responded that she would see what she would do.

We had dinner within the week. After a glass or two of very excellent wine, I felt sufficiently fortified to plunge into the purpose for the dinner. I told him about the power line technology, told him it worked, and told him that Palumbo's team was not moving fast enough. (If this technology really worked, it could enable AT&T to bypass the local exchange companies all together. In other words, no more access charges!) Then I delivered my recommendation: give the project to me! I told him that the project boiled down to finding someone who could negotiate deals with the power companies. Modesty and good wine don't mix, and I laid out my case for telling him that I was as good a negotiator as he had in AT&T!

I didn't hear anything for a couple of days, and then Marie called me to let me know that the next morning Dorman was doing a tour of the lab where they had the power line demo. I joined him and listened as Hossein explained the technology. Dorman gave me a wink during the presentation, but other than that, we didn't have much of a chance to speak. It didn't matter; the fact that he was interacting with the scientists, the fact that he was there at all, made me want to walk through fire for him. His mind seemed as open to new ideas as Armstrong's had seemed closed.

Two days later, I received two calls: the first was from Marie, telling me that Dorman had asked me to be on the agenda for the next Executive Committee meeting, where I should be prepared to discuss the business plan for the power lines project. (The Executive Committee was the most senior deliberative body at AT&T, comprised of the Chairman and his direct reports.) The second call was from Jim Cicconi, my boss, telling me that Dorman had told him to do what was necessary to free me up for a special project. We agreed that I would continue to report to Cicconi, but I asked – and he agreed – to use this opportunity to replace me as the chief lawyer for Business Services.

I had never done a business plan before. My first draft proposed that we spend ten billion dollars in order to serve about a hundred million homes and small businesses. It seemed conservative to me, given that we had spent over one hundred billion dollars trying to do the same thing with cable television. Fortunately, I shared this with a few people who were more used to the budget process, who gave me sage advice to come in with a smaller number. The important thing, they said, was to get the green light and get started. Then, when you were up and running, you could come back in and ask for more. The whole thing reminded me of Teddy Roosevelt's tactic when Congress only appropriated half the money necessary to send the U.S. fleet around the world. He sent the fleet halfway around the world, and then told Congress it was up to them to decide whether to bring the fleet back.

My budget in my second draft was about one percent of the budget in the first draft. But that was still about one hundred million dollars. I was told again that I didn't understand how to do these things. Was that really what I needed, stripped to its essentials, to get started?

By the time I made the presentation I had reduced the proposed budget to five million dollars. Most of that was to fund a study by an expert to beat back a challenge of ham radio operators who claimed use of power lines in the way AT&T wanted to so would interfere with the use of spectrum by ham radio operators. (It wouldn't.) The proposal and budget were approved, and I naively thought I was off and running. I had not counted on the active obstructionist tactics of the Consumer Leadership group, who felt stung by my taking over what they thought they had been doing perfectly well. Their tactics included everything from boycotting meetings to refusing to release the funds approved by the Executive Committee, claiming that their process, even for budgets approved by the Chairman, was to circulate a written document and obtain the signatures of their "Board" before releasing a single penny. It took them three months to collect the necessary signatures, even though their offices were all located together, on the same floor of the same building.

I had no money and no staff. I borrowed on a full time basis Steve Sobolovich, who had been the strategic pricing director for Business Services and who, for my money, was the most knowledgeable and best negotiator within AT&T.[74] And, I was able to borrow people from every organization except from Consumer.[75] I borrowed Vicki Fleiss from my old legal group. I have to admit it was a delightful experience to be the client, giving vague guidance as to what I had decided on some point and telling Vicki to "write it up," which she would do quite successfully. With my wonderful and loyal secretary Pat Oakes rounding out the crew, I was completely satisfied with the team I could deploy.

The work was straightforward. I worked with suppliers of the necessary electronics to make certain that the development would match our deployment schedule, worked with others who were sticking their

---

74 The strategic pricing director had the unenviable task of policing the sales teams who constantly wanted to give price and non-price terms that might win a particular customer but would be bad for the business. Sales teams were not paid to see the big picture, but to win their assigned customers, and the friction could become intense.

75 There was one exception within the Consumer team. Dan Hall, who had just recently come to AT&T and thought getting things done was more important than politics, helped from day one.

toes in the water using power lines, and finally, began a dance with a number of power companies to see which ones would make suitable partners. Most of the power companies were very conservative in approach, having been spooked by Enron and the scandals that hit those power companies that had been involved with it. Still, there were some prepared to take the risk of being first into new territory if they had a partner like AT&T. I found what I thought was the right partner and began negotiating a suitable framework agreement – something that would enable us to go public with an early success while still haggling over the minor details. After a few fits and starts, we negotiated to conclusion a short agreement that would commit each of us to build out a system in a major southern city, sharing the costs of doing so on a 50-50 basis, while giving AT&T primacy on all marketing decisions with respect to the marketing of telecom services over the powerline infrastructure. Even had we paid all of the costs, the service had a lower cost structure than what we knew of the incumbent local company costs; by cutting those costs in half, we would have been in a strong position to win local customers.

I realized that we would need an offer to convince customers to use the service, and I also was concerned that the Consumer team would do next to nothing to market our service via power lines. I was fretting about this on a plane coming back from an industry conference that Sobolovich and I had attended when I started playing around with some ideas. By the time the plane landed I had sketched out a very interesting marketing approach. Once back at headquarters, I was explaining how it would work to some of my attorney friends, when one – a patent attorney – spoke up, saying that he thought the idea was patentable and that if I were willing to sit down and explain it to him in detail he would see what he could do. And that is how Patent No. 7,573,992 B1 (issued August 11, 2009) came about. Though I am listed as the inventor, I assigned all rights to the patent to AT&T – the norm for intellectual property created by employees. Unfortunately, the idea is buried in the papers of an abandoned project, and is unlikely to ever be used.

In any event, once the power company representative and I had agreed on text of our agreement, I sent Dorman a note reporting our success. I also let him know that our partner, a highly respected utility with a large base of operations throughout the south, wanted to announce our cooperation. Dorman put me on the Executive Committee Agenda. At the meeting, I started to describe the deal when Hossein interrupted, saying he had new reservations about the technology. I looked at the folks from AT&T Labs who were there and they shrugged, their faces telling me that this was news to them. Next, Bill Hannigan, who Dorman had brought in to run Business Services and I regarded as both a friend and a straight shooter, spoke up saying that he was concerned that we had the market lead here, because if this were so good, someone else would be pouring money into it already.

I made a response to both points, but knew something was up, because neither of the comments made much sense, and both came from people whose judgments I normally would respect. I was told that afternoon the project was dead, and without knowing all of the answers, I began making the necessary calls to disappointed suppliers and partners that AT&T would not be proceeding on the power line project after all.

I had my own suspicions about the real reason AT&T pulled the plug on the power line project. I requested another dinner meeting with Dorman, who confirmed privately what I had begun to believe: among ideas to save the company, power lines had been plan B. There were too many unanswered questions to adopt it in lieu of plan A, which had been to sell the Company. Dorman needed to shut down the power line project in order to simplify the process for regulatory approval of Plan A, because if the regulators thought AT&T had a viable alternative to merging with an RBOC, they would have been less likely to approve a merger, especially one with SBC. I laid all of this out to him and he smiled and nodded in the affirmative. At least now I had a reason. As I recall, we had a very nice dinner.

Chapter 24

The End: SBC Buys AT&T

AT&T had emerged from divestiture in 1984 with one problem — access charges — but a lot going for it. It was still a very wealthy corporation with tremendous cash flow and a business capable of generating healthy profits for the foreseeable future.

Twenty years later, the company was in serious trouble. It had not solved the access problem either politically, technologically, or in the marketplace, and thanks to Mike Armstrong, had squandered virtually all of its capital, and had gutted its core business to the point that there was little hope of surviving the coming onslaught from the RBOCs in long distance.

SBC had a much more humble beginning. At the time of divestiture, sixty percent of its revenue came from a single state – Texas. The other places SBC operated – Kansas, Missouri, Oklahoma, and Arkansas – are fine places as well, but generally not the first places one would pick to live if one had the choice. Most people were choosing to live in fast-growing states like California. And because communications revenues follow the people, markets like Oklahoma and Arkansas, while respectable, were not the top growth markets one would expect to spawn the next telecom king of the hill.

And yet it was SBC that came out on top, buying not only Pacific Telesis (serving California, Arizona and Hawaii); Ameritech (serving the Midwest, including Illinois, Michigan and Ohio), Bell South, serving the nine southern states, and AT&T. This is a testament to the management of that company, not to any God-given advantages. Their strategies and execution simply were better than those demonstrated by the other companies (including AT&T), and as a result they survived.

SBC was not the only partner considered by AT&T. AT&T had serious discussions with Bell South between 2002 and 2004. Dave Dorman had started talking to Bell South even before he became CEO. In fact, Armstrong had sent Chuck Noski, the AT&T Chief Financial Officer, to Bell South's Atlanta headquarters to begin discussions. Noski was shocked to discover that Dorman (at the time President of AT&T) had already been there and had initiated discussions on his own!

The first round of discussions came to a screeching halt when an AT&T attorney leaked word of the talks. Bell South's stock took a pounding, and its Chairman pulled the plug on any further discussions at that time. In the summer of 2004, however, the talks resumed and seemed to make great progress. Bell South in fact was doing its due diligence review of AT&T's operations when the talks hit another snag. The issue was Business Services; there was recognition by both parties that absent an RBOC partner, AT&T's consumer business had little value. The services offered to consumers were not differentiated, and because of access charges that AT&T had to pay, its cost structure was not cost-competitive. Business Services was less vulnerable, especially with the large customers whose networks did not depend on switched access, and had large amounts of data. These customers remained loyal to AT&T in part because the cable companies were non-players, and the RBOCs were not yet ready to take AT&T on in data networking.

Yet, the damage done by Armstrong had the traditional business reeling. Dorman was very active attempting repairs, but the business was still struggling. Dorman, now the AT&T CEO, wanted to present a rosy forecast for the coming year to keep Bell South interested. Betsy

Bernard, who had been hired by Dorman to head the consumer unit when the plan had been to spin it off, and then took over Business Services when Dorman was promoted to Chairman, wanted no part of it. She would be the one responsible for making the forecast if she agreed to it, and she didn't want to agree to targets that were not supported by plans on how to get there. As a result, Dorman banished her from the discussions. She left the company a short while later.

Bernard's absence from the talks roused Bell South's suspicions. The other AT&T executive who had extensive dealings with Bell South was Barb Peda. She had braved substantial internal infighting to gain the right to supply Bell South's nascent long distance enterprise long distance capacity on a wholesale basis. Yes, they were fighting us to win the retail business, but her thinking agreed to by Noski was that it was better to keep some portion of the customer's business, albeit a smaller wholesaler's portion, than lose it all. Bell South asked for her participation in the discussions but Dorman kept her away. I asked Cicconi why, and his response was that they were not certain that Peda would play the party line rather than be loyal to Bernard. In other words, they were concerned about her integrity and the fact that she might give an honest appraisal of the state of the business. Being kept from talking to the operational leaders of the business made the ever-cautious Bell South more cautious still. Whether or not the talks were salvageable at that point is unclear. The parties were apart on price and could not bridge the gap. The talks with Bell South ended.

Bell South had not been the best potential partner in any event. It was very conservative, almost to the point that it seemed uncomfortable with divestiture. Unlike SBC, who had expanded aggressively outside its original territory through acquisitions of Pacific Telesis and Ameritech, Bell South had started life serving customers in nine states, and had not expanded at all. So why shouldn't AT&T do something with SBC? The two companies had held discussions at an earlier point. Reed Hundt, the Chairman of the Federal Communications

Commission at the time, had termed a merger between the two "unthinkable." Because approval of the FCC would be necessary, along with that of the Department of Justice, this cool reception to the idea had a chilling effect on serious discussions until Hundt left and Michael Powell came in as the new FCC chairman. Powell didn't think competition between the long distance carriers and the local carriers made sense, and had done a good job of stacking the deck in the local carriers' favor. Given that stance, the parties guessed correctly that he would readily approve a merger between the two.

The beginning of the discussion with SBC that resulted in the acquisition occurred at an industry conference held under the auspices of the FCC to try to resolve the access issue. The notion that the issue could be resolved in a manner satisfactory to all was plain silly; this was not a problem with a win-win solution. Also, the local exchange industry knew that in the absence of a deal, Powell would continue on a course that was favorable to them. Yet the CEOs of both AT&T, SBC, and many others, had been sent invitations to attend the conference, and they didn't feel comfortable refusing. With the CEOs from both AT&T and SBC there, and with both believing that the purported topic was a waste of time, they needed something to do. That something was to begin talking about re-shaping the industry through a merger.

The discussions were not completely smooth. In any transaction of this size, and especially where you are merging two previously separate entities, there are in fact two negotiations that take place. The first negotiation is the deal to buy the billions of dollars of assets, which is of great interest to both sets of shareholders. The second and often more critical negotiation is to determine which executives stay, and which executives go. For those who go, it also must be decided how much they receive as severance. Not infrequently, deals of great interest to the shareholders are not done because an executive is not personally satisfied with the role he will have once the deal is done, or, if he will have no role, the amount of severance he will be given.

Here, Dave Dorman let it be known during the talks that he wanted to come into the merged company as the successor to SBC's CEO Ed Whitacre, something Whitacre was unwilling to accept. The message was conveyed back to Dorman that he was not wanted and would have no role in the merged company. Whitacre was more receptive to the number two executive at AT&T, Bill Hannigan. The two discussed Hannigan staying on as a candidate to succeed Whitacre. Hannigan declined, in part because he did not want to move his family to Texas, and in part because he knew, even if he stayed on, he would have an uphill battle against more established internal candidates for the top job.

Dorman, to his credit, continued to pursue a deal with SBC, even though he would be forced out once the deal was done. Instead, he sought and obtained a hefty severance payment to palliate his wounded ego.

Normally, when companies are acquired, they obtain a premium over their pre-existing stock price in order to induce their shareholders to accept the deal. No premium was offered for AT&T. The offer, at the then-prevailing price for AT&T shares, translated to about sixteen billion dollars. The price seems absurdly low for a company with over thirty-one billion dollars in annual revenues, but was it? The price reflected the almost unanimous consensus that the company was cornered, without real hopes for the future. Those who criticize the price *as too low* do not understand the disaster looming for the company. AT&T faced a liquidity crisis as a result of Armstrong's spending hysteria that had forced it to spin-off wireless (because this capital intensive business could not attract capital as long as it was attached to the long-distance enterprise) and to sell its cable interests (to reduce in part the debt AT&T had accumulated in buying them). The only thing left was the traditional long distance business, the worse for being squeezed for every penny of capital by Armstrong, and facing an impossible cost advantage enjoyed by its RBOC rivals due to FCC policy.

In fact, the real issue was whether SBC wasn't paying too much! Those on the SBC Board who opposed the deal did so on this ground, stating that they weren't opposed to buying AT&T, but that if SBC just waited another year or two, they could get it for next to nothing. Once again, though, SBC had calculated correctly. Whitacre convinced his Board that waiting might lower the price, but it would also lower the value of that which it was buying. The brand and remaining assets would be adversely affected by continued deterioration of the company – key employees would continue to leave to find places to work with futures, customers would continue to defect, etc. The SBC Board approved the transaction, and the combined enterprise hasn't looked back.

The AT&T Board had greater problems with the deal. The sticking points with some Board members were the absence of a premium, and Dorman's severance package. While the Board ultimately approved the deal, the approval was not unanimous and came after interminable debate, lasting until three o'clock in the morning the day the deal was announced.

For a company who had bought IBM's Global Network for five billion dollars and TCG for more than eleven billion dollars, the sixteen billion dollar price tag for all of AT&T, including whatever was left of the IBM global network and TCG, was a glaring indictment of the way AT&T had been managed. TCG and the IBM global network together now represented less than 5% of AT&T's revenues, and none of its profits (since neither was profitable). Yet AT&T had paid as much for them as SBC was now paying for all of AT&T! Although the mismanagement had occurred prior to Dorman's taking over, he was disliked by some members of the Board for profiting personally through the sale of the company. There is no denying that he was richly rewarded for selling the company. His severance agreement was structured so that he could retire as an officer of the newly merged company, doubling his pension to about two million a year. He also received a severance payment of between thirty-five and fifty-five million dollars, as well as another 400,000 shares in exchange for a three year consulting contract with the new company (worth about eight million dollars at the time it was given), which was not interested in availing itself of his help.

Despite the largess he was able to negotiate for himself, I believe the criticism of Dorman is misplaced. Did he assume the top job at AT&T, intending to sell the company? Probably. Did he do so on terms that enriched him personally? Definitely. So why the favorable review?

Dorman knew the industry and made few blunders as Chairman. Though much more knowledgeable than Armstrong, he was also far less arrogant – he would listen to contrary views and change his mind if he were persuaded. It is not his fault that Armstrong had stripped AT&T of any realistic hopes of survival as an independent company. Barring a miracle, the only hope left was to sell the company, and the fact that he recognized this and acted quickly saved jobs and shareholder value. True, AT&T was sold without a premium, but it is difficult to conclude that AT&T's business would have done anything other than continue to deteriorate. AT&T was on a precipice, with neither time, money, wireless or cable assets, nor a viable business strategy to combat the cost advantage access charges gave the RBOCs. Where was growth going to come from?

By selling quickly, those with shares in a dying company became shareholders in one of the most powerful telecom companies in the market. Though it is difficult to draw irrefutable conclusions because of the market volatility, it is at least true on the broadest level that the value of a shareholding in the merged company has gone up more than fifty percent in the five years after the deal, which is almost certainly better than the shareholders would have done without the deal.

Dorman's severance package was a lot of money. Unlike the other executives I've discussed in this book (Armstrong, McGinn, Hindrey, and Walters), Dorman received his as a result of orchestrating something (the sale of the company) that benefited shareholders, not just himself. He played out the cards he was dealt with grace and style, and sold the company after concluding, in my opinion rationally, that there were no better alternatives. Compared to the actions of his predecessor, he acted with sheer genius in stopping the continued slide of the company.

Today, AT&T no longer exists. Oh, you can say it does, and SBC certainly pretends that it is the same company. It calls itself AT&T, as it has the right to do since it bought the rights to the name in 2005. It also brags about the eight Nobel prizes the company won. It certainly is large enough to emulate its namesake and pioneer new ways to communicate: it has more than 360,000 employees and about one hundred and thirty billion dollars in revenue.

But the heart and soul of the company are different. The spirit of public service is no longer there. In place of the former public-service mentality is the more traditional got-to-make-profits mentality that is honorable but different.

The single-minded pursuit of profits will not sustain the kind of investments in research that made AT&T the national treasure that it was – the kind of place that generated so much pioneering work and generated those eight Nobel prizes. Personally, my brain is just not nimble enough to look at the current AT&T and see the old Ma Bell, the cantankerous but brilliant monopolist who brought us more lasting value through its inventions and discoveries than any other corporation in history!

From the added perspective of one who cares about this country and its place in the world, there is the added pain of realizing how many jobs this country lost. These losses were not only for the provision of telecom service and equipment to those in the U.S., where the numbers of employees is down several hundred thousand from what AT&T employed in the early 1980s, but also the jobs that could have been added to the economy had the government helped rather than made it as difficult as possible (including making it illegal for several decades) for the company to sell what it invented around the world.

It is ironic but beyond serious dispute that the Republican party, normally thought of as being more hospitable to business, was the political force that was in power when virtually every bad thing done to AT&T by government was done – from entering the 1956 decree that stripped the company of its technological advantages, to forcing the break-up of the company, to the FCC's final denouement, using access charges to finally destroy what was left of the wounded giant. It also seems to be the party that puts abstract ideas (like its misguided belief in free trade) above business pragmatism and helping U.S. companies survive. I say this not to advance any set of political views, but because it is true, at least historically, in this one case.

Afterward

AT&T must accept responsibility for its own doom, having made what I called the four "Colossal Failures." They were: (1) the agreement by the Company to the 1956 Decree, pursuant to which the company was forced to give to the world without compensation its entire patent portfolio, including patents to such things as the transistor, the laser, digital signal processors, and solar cells; (2) the decision in 1971 not to accept the U.S. government's offer to take over "Arpanet," the early name for what has become the Internet; (3) the agreement of the Company in 1982 to a change to the Modification of Final Judgment it had negotiated with the Department of Justice, which gave AT&T's wireless licenses and business to the Regional Bell Operating Companies; and (4) the failure by the Company in 1997 to find the right Chief Executive Officer to lead the Company at a critical time. Change any one of those mistakes and you'd probably still have an independent, healthy AT&T.

It is also true that the government figured prominently in two of those decisions (numbers one and three), and took advantage of the fourth to kill the company. To review the history of these mistakes, made one after the other, is depressing business. It would be less depressing if we learned from the mistakes made and did what was possible to avoid their repetition. The following is my list of what I optimistically call "lessons learned," I hope people take from this book.

1. In the right circumstances, a government-regulated monopoly can be more desirable than competition.

This country went through a painful transition in a number of industries from regulated monopolies to deregulated private companies supposedly competing with each other. In retrospect, in some industries it may not have been such a great idea. It is hard to look at the wonderful record of innovation and invention compiled by the Bell System and conclude that it was a bad way to run things. AT&T did best as a regulated monopoly, and delivered the best, most innovative, lowest cost service of any provider anywhere in the world. Under these circumstances, it is hard to conclude that we are always better off with a competitive model than a regulated one. Maximizing profits as a single-minded goal doesn't always bring out the behavior we want, particularly if the conditions are inhospitable for competition.

We don't know enough at this point to be able to delineate a set of conditions that mitigate in the direction of competition or regulated monopoly. What is clear that in industry after industry we have abandoned the regulated monopoly approach in favor of competition, with very mixed results. We would be better off if we approached each industry with fact-based analysis and without pre-ordained dogmas (such as competition is always better).

2. Shareholders Need Greater Protection from Inept Executives and Corporate Boards.

In theory, corporations are democratically managed. Shareholders elect the Boards of Directors, and in turn, the Board oversees the Chief Executive Officer, replacing him when they feel he is not doing his job well. In fact, corporate governance has few similarities to the theory. Boards of Directors are dysfunctional at best, filled with individuals for whom the Board is a part time function, done in addition to their real jobs. They frequently are friends of the CEO, because it is management that in almost all instances comes up with proposed Board Members.

AT&T is Exhibit 1 to the proof that our current Boards do not work. Bob Allen may not have been right for the job of changing the company, but at least he didn't make any serious mistakes. In contrast, Mike Armstrong was an absolute disaster, coming time and again to the Board for authority to make absurd deals. Yet, Business Week reported that in December 2000, when the full extent of the disaster caused by Armstrong's profligate spending was already apparent, and the damage done to its traditional business had been disclosed sending the stock into a tailspin, the Board of Directors gave Armstrong a standing ovation at his performance review! To read that even now is upsetting, because I was on the front lines, watching as thousands of fellow employees were laid off in order to squeeze the last dollar of profits from our traditional business, so that our chairman could be taken to the cleaners in deal after deal!

Being a member of a Board must be viewed as a serious vocation, not a part-time job. The way to change this would be to change state law to (1) limit the number of Board members, thus making certain that each Board member is accountable; (2) prescribe that members of the Board make serious compensation; and (3) that they also face serious financial exposure if they fail to take action after management repeatedly leads the company into the ditch. Finally, I would set up an independent panel, staffed by respected members of the business community, to review Board nominations and perhaps make some of its own from time to time. This last proposal should help break the cozy relationship between boards and senior managers. Finally, something should be done, again at the state law level, to limit the severance payments to executives to something reasonable, say, no more than six months compensation. It isn't right that the same executives who acted to eliminate pensions for their employees (as happened at

AT&T), negotiated for themselves severance payments worth tens of millions of dollars (as also happened). Six months pay seems generous, especially when one considers the two weeks pay most employees receive when let go.

3. At a Minimum, We Should Hold Our Members of Congress to the Same Ethical Standards We Expect of Foreign Officials.

Congress has made it a crime for a U.S. company to give something of value to a foreign official for the purpose of obtaining or retaining business. Congress has not passed anything requiring similar conduct of itself, or of any other officials within the United States. This is hypocrisy at its worst. Very simply, it is a subversion of the free market to tolerate Members of Congress interfering in governmental procurement decisions on behalf of companies who have given them money. It is also unethical and can only result in higher prices and lower quality than would be the case if public procurements were conducted solely on the basis of merit, without political interference. This is, to use a colloquial expression, a "no-brainer."

4. The Country Should Stop Practicing "Teenage Economics."

This country has a deep and abiding belief that the role of government is to maximize the health of consumers. Our trade policies and antitrust enforcement are all based on that belief. We assume, based on various theories, that if we do that, the rest of the economy will take care of itself. Well, I am here to tell you that the theories are incorrect.

The reason I call it teenage economics is because teenagers assume there will always be money to spend without worrying where it comes from. So, as a society, do we. Let me introduce one more label to you and then I'll get to work telling you what I mean. "Producers" is my name for all of those entities that provide the consumers what they consume. AT&T was a producer. So is IBM, GE, a doctor, a super-market, etc. Healthy producers are also the source of well-paying jobs, so that consumers can spend the money they earn.

Recently, though, many of those jobs have vanished. Many of the jobs lost have gone overseas. Some of them should have. Others, however, have moved because other governments have industrial policies while our government thinks it doesn't need one, believing instead in "free trade." I remember too clearly that AT&T, who made the best telecom equipment in the world, could not sell into France or Germany because those markets were not open, to be a real enthusiast for free trade. I also remember our sales efforts being thwarted elsewhere because we wouldn't match our competitors' willingness to pay bribes. And finally, I remember my disgust when I read that Alcatel, a former competitor headquartered in France, bought Lucent – including Bell Labs!

Those memories prevent me from believing in free trade. I see no reason that this experience is unique to me, and I suspect that inquiry would produce a patchwork of other key markets where U.S. companies were first boxed out of foreign markets and then taken over. If that is so, it explains where many of those well-paying jobs are going.

I don't want to ignite a trade war, but neither do I believe that those who naively preach about free trade have some insight that I lack. Ignorance of reality rarely produces insights worth a damn. What I do believe is that market access is a tremendously valuable asset that we need to learn to manage, not because it helps U.S. consumers, but because it is vital if we are to protect U.S. producers and U.S. jobs. Economic survival requires more than lip service to empty slogans. We need to do a far better job of clearing out foreign government meddling to help their own companies before we can withdraw and let the "free" market operate.

AT&T spent billions of dollars trying to gain access to foreign markets, and never succeeded. Yet, access to the U.S. market is given away routinely because of our philosophical beliefs. I worked eight years supporting AT&T's international efforts, and never encountered a fact situation consistent with the existence of free trade. That is not to say that the U.S. ought to start blocking market access, but neither does it make sense to give it away for free to rich companies who use their own protected home markets, and bribes in other countries, to destroy American business. That's not policy; that's stupidity. Policy is choosing whether to harvest the value of market access on behalf of taxpayers (by charging for such access directly) or to use it on behalf of U.S. based producers (by conditioning access to U.S. markets on equivalent access for U.S. producers in their home markets).

5. What the heck are they teaching in business schools anyway?

It's clear that so many of the players in the tragi-comedy that was AT&T's fall from grace were in over their heads and could not make wise decisions. Yet most had strong credentials from "good" schools. We ought to try something different.

Mike Armstrong had one admirable quality among a host of bad ones. He was decisive. That's good. His problem was that he constantly made poor decisions because he was both ignorant of some of the key value drivers in the industry, and was too arrogant to assume anything he didn't know could make a difference. If there were an elixir that could replace arrogance with common sense, the maker of such a wonderful cocktail could name his price. In its absence, perhaps one of the schools that turned out such duds could instead come up with a means to screen for the sort of qualities that we know from experience make either good, or bad, CEOs. I'm dead serious. We measure all sorts of aptitudes: why is it that we can't measure levels of open-mindedness or willing to listen, on the one hand, and arrogance on the other? We could do no worse than the current batch of idiots we turn over our corporations to manage.

6. Finally, we should do something to restore a "Labs" as a haven for pure research.

The greatest sense of loss in this entire story is the loss of Bell Labs. I don't know if it is possible to bring it back, divorced from a private company that stands ready to use what it comes up with. But we ought to try. If this country could generate a small fraction of the ideas and inventions the Labs generated, licensed for reasonable fees to all U.S. employers, then we would have to consider the money well spent. The funding would not need to come from taxpayers. How about using charges for market access to the United States to generate money for such a national resource? In other words, companies that made their products overseas, be they U.S. or foreign owned, would pay a one percent fee to import those products into the U.S., in addition to whatever duties now apply. Can you imagine how much a one percent duty on all imports would generate? Tens of billions of dollars each year! Now imagine a national research laboratory that pursued exploration in the worlds of physics, chemistry, and human health!

It wouldn't make this whole history seem worth it, but it would help.

CPSIA information can be obtained at www.ICGtesting.com
Printed in the USA
LVOW01s1300160114

369684LV00003B/589/P